PUB STROLLS IN
HAMPSHIRE
& THE NEW FOREST

Anne-Marie Edwards

COUNTRYSIDE BOOKS
NEWBURY BERKSHIRE

First published 2000
© Anne-Marie Edwards 2000

Revised and updated 2003, 2006

COUNTRYSIDE BOOKS
3 Catherine Road
Newbury, Berkshire

To view our complete range of books,
please visit us at
www.countrysidebooks.co.uk

ISBN 1 85306 618 4
EAN 978185306 6184

For our daughter, Julie

Designed by Graham Whiteman
Photographs by Mike Edwards
Maps by Gelder design & mapping

Produced through MRM Associates Ltd., Reading
Printed in Singapore

Contents

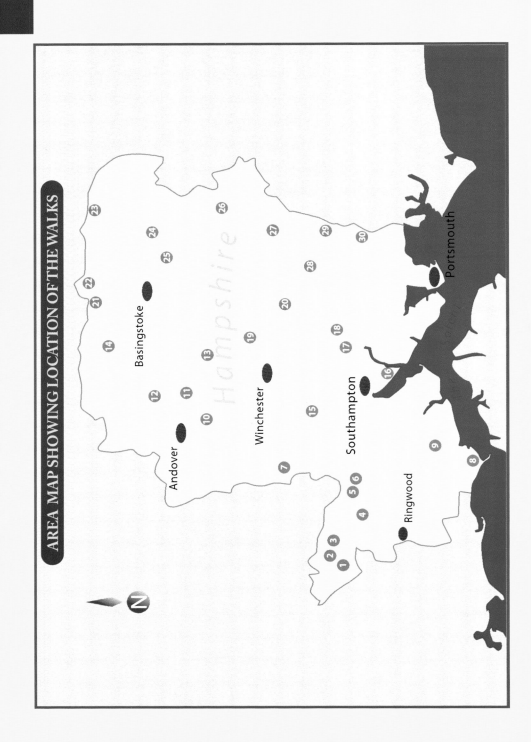

AREA MAP SHOWING LOCATION OF THE WALKS

WALK

PUBLISHER'S NOTE

We hope that you obtain considerable enjoyment from this book; great care has been taken in its preparation. However, changes of landlord and actual closures are sadly not uncommon. Likewise, although at the time of publication all routes followed public rights of ways or permitted paths, diversion orders can be made and permissions withdrawn.

We cannot, of course, be held responsible for such diversion orders and any inaccuracies in the text which result from these or any other changes to the routes nor any damage which might result from walkers trespassing on private property. We are anxious though that all details covering the walks and the pubs are kept up to date and would therefore welcome information from readers which would be relevant to future editions.

The sketch maps accompanying each walk are not always to scale and are intended to guide you to the starting point and give a simple but accurate idea of the route to be taken. For those who like the benefit of detailed maps, we recommend that you arm yourself with relevant Ordnance Survey map in the Pathfinder, Outdoor Leisure or Explorer series.

This is a book of walks with a difference! All of the thirty strolls are short but they are carefully planned to enable everyone, including families with small children, the not-so-fit and the not-so-young, to enjoy the best of Hampshire's beautiful country-side. There are many treasures to discover in this splendidly varied county and you do not need to walk far to find them.

Hampshire is a county of contrasts. In the west, extending southwards from the Wiltshire downs to the Solent, is the unique medieval landscape of the New Forest, over 100 square miles of heathland, lawns, and ancient oak and beech woods. We leave the busy centres to walk in some of the Forest's loveliest places and discover more about its history and fascinating wildlife.

Hampshire's coastline fringes the Solent for over 70 miles and a surprisingly large extent remains wild and undeveloped. I have chosen rambles in the bird-haunted marshes around Keyhaven and Pennington and Hamble's delightful Common fringing the estuary of its famous river.

Rolling chalk downland forms the heart of the county, rising in the north-west to create the beautiful hills known as 'The Hampshire Highlands'. Here we follow ways in the Bourne valley once frequented by Jane Austen and William Cobbett. Close to the Sussex border the South Downs reach their most westerly point, descending abruptly to the greensand rocks of the Weald and creating a dramatic landscape characterised by steep, densely-wooded hillsides known as 'hangers'. This wonderful walking country forms the setting for exciting strolls around Buriton,

an enchanting village built of local cream-coloured malmstone, and Hawkley tucked away in a secret valley.

Rising in the chalk, Hampshire's main rivers, the Test, the Itchen and the Meon, flow gently southwards, carving wide valleys in the downs. We follow riverside paths to visit more of Hampshire's attractive villages, including Wherwell, its streets lined with thatched and timber-framed houses leading to the remains of an abbey founded by the Saxon Queen Elfrida, East Meon with its wonderful Norman church and medieval Court House and Itchen Abbas where Charles Kingsley wrote part of *The Water Babies* and Lord Grey of Falloden loved to fish.

Although these walks are short (between $1^1/_4$ and 3 miles) they are long enough to justify a visit to a good pub! All the routes are circular and start at, or close to, an excellent pub chosen for its home-cooking and welcoming atmosphere. There are details of what food and drink are available, together with opening times and telephone numbers. (Opening times may be affected by the new regulations and the beers on offer are frequently varied.) All the publicans I spoke to were happy to allow patrons to leave cars while they walk but they do ask you to seek their permission first.

For help in checking the walks for this reprint, I am most grateful to Margaret and Ian Knowles, our daughter Julie, and Richard and his friends. Happy strolling!

Anne-Marie Edwards

Rockbourne
The Rose and Thistle

MAP: OS OUTDOOR LEISURE 22 (GR 114184) **WALK 1** **DISTANCE:** 2½ MILES

DIRECTIONS TO START: ROCKBOURNE IS 4 MILES NORTH-WEST OF FORDINGBRIDGE. TURN OFF THE B3078 BETWEEN FORDINGBRIDGE AND CRANBORNE. DRIVE THROUGH ROCKBOURNE TO THE VILLAGE HALL WHICH IS ON THE LEFT WITH CLEAR CAR PARK SIGNS. **PARKING:** THE PUB CAR PARK IS SMALL SO BEGIN THIS WALK FROM THE LARGE CAR PARK BEHIND THE VILLAGE HALL AS INDICATED ABOVE.

When it came to finding a place to live, the Romans, who settled in Britain after the invasion of AD 43, always chose wisely. Near present-day Rockbourne they found all they required. Here was a beautiful valley in a fold of the downs, watered by a clear chalk stream, with enough fertile land for their crops, good grazing for their animals and south-facing slopes for their vines. This is a walk in their footsteps. From Rockbourne, with its timber-framed thatched houses, ancient manor and early Norman church, the route follows the valley to visit the remains of the Roman Villa. A short downland climb is rewarded by splendid views before we return to the village.

The Rose and Thistle

The 16th century Rose and Thistle was originally two cottages. One cottage forms the bar area which has barrel chairs and stools and the other a pleasant dining room with enormous fireplaces and comfortable wooden settles. Beers on offer when we called were London Pride, Morrells Oxford Bitter and Summer Lightning. The menu is extensive, ranging from home-made sausages to venison served with chestnuts and spring onions. A good selection of wines is available.

Opening times on Monday to Saturday are from 11 am to 3 pm and from 6 pm to 11 pm and on Sunday from 12 noon to 3 pm and 7 pm to 10.30 pm. Food is served from 12 noon to 2 pm and from 7 pm to 9.30 pm. Children are welcome and dogs are allowed in the garden and bar area. Telephone: 01725 518236.

The Walk

① Cross the road in front of the village hall and to the right of a phone box turn left along a gravel track. Pass a house on your right and take the narrow footpath a little to the left signed 'To the Church'. This brings you to a wide gravel area in front of Manor Farm. Cross the gravel and turn right up the steps to the church. A small gate on the left admits you to the churchyard. The beautifully cared for church is well worth a visit. As you leave the church turn right across the grass to look down on Manor Farm which incorporates some medieval buildings including a 14th century chapel.

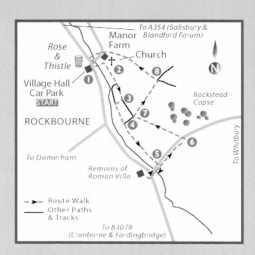

② Retrace your steps through the gate and turn left along a grassy path, church on your left. When this becomes gravelled keep straight on with trees, then views of the valley, on your right.

③ In about ¹/₂ mile you cross a stile. Turn right down some steps and through a gate to walk downhill with a fence on your right. At the foot of the field turn left (do not cross the stile) and keep ahead, still with a fence on your right. Continue through gates beside the fence until you come to a stile on your right. Cross this and turn left to resume your former heading with the fence and hedge now on your left. Go over a stile and cross a little orchard in front of a thatched house. Another stile brings you to a track in front of Marsh Farm.

④ Continue along the path to the left of the entrance, passing Marsh Farm on your right, and keep ahead through gates and over stiles to an asphalt lane.

⑤ Turn right down the lane to a road and bear right for a few yards to the entrance to

Rockbourne Roman villa.

the Roman Villa on the left. After your visit, return to the road and turn right, then left to retrace your steps up the lane. Follow the lane uphill for about ¹/₄ mile towards Rockstead Copse.

⑥ Just before you come to the trees look carefully for a stile and footpath sign on the left. Cross the stile and walk over the field ahead to the corner of a finger of woodland. Keep ahead with the trees on your right, then follow the path which dips over a field and crosses a low bank by a

PLACES OF INTEREST NEARBY

Rockbourne Roman Villa was one of the largest in southern Britain. Open daily from 1st April to 1st October weekdays 12 noon to 6 pm. Weekends and July and August 10.30 am to 6 pm. Tel: 01725 518541.

Manor Farm sign. The narrow footpath ahead brings you over a stile to a wide grassy crossing path.

⑦ Turn right to follow a splendid downland way which climbs to give wonderful views over the rooftops of Rockbourne tucked snugly in the valley below. After about ¹/₄ mile the path dips to meet a crossing gravel track.

⑧ Turn left and follow the track as it leads downhill over a cattle grid and becomes a lane curving left towards Manor Farm. Go through the gate in front of some of the farm buildings and bear a little right to continue with the wall surrounding Manor Farm on your left to the road. Turn right for a few yards for the Rose and Thistle or left to return to your car.

Damerham
The Compasses Inn

MAP: OS OUTDOOR LEISURE 22 (GR 104162)   **WALK 2**   **DISTANCE:** 2 MILES

DIRECTIONS TO START: DAMERHAM IS BESIDE THE B3078 ABOUT 3 MILES WEST OF FORDINGBRIDGE. **PARKING:** PATRONS MAY LEAVE THEIR CARS AT THE PUB WHILE THEY WALK – PLEASE ASK FIRST.

Damerham is an old world village beautifully set beside a network of tiny streams in the valley of the river Allen. The houses and farms are so scattered that each part of the village has its own name. As you walk from North End through East End to South End, houses appear unexpectedly, half-hidden in a fold of the downs or lost among the oak woods. The intervening country is wild and marshy crossed by causeways and wooden footbridges, reminiscent of the Everglades. So I think you will find this walk exciting and different. Wear strong shoes and be prepared to tackle the odd muddy patch.

The Compasses Inn

A village as interesting as Damerham must have a good pub and you will not be disappointed. The Compasses Inn is outstanding. It has been an inn for over 400 years and at one time was virtually self-sufficient with its own brewery, coach house, dairy, well and butchery. The old brew tower is still standing and it is said that a phantom coach drives into the coach house on stormy nights! For 600 years the Manor of Damerham belonged to Glastonbury Abbey and the manorial court continued to be held at the Compasses until 1920. Scenes of village life in the past decorate both bars and the very pleasant dining room overlooks the garden and the downs.

Four real ales are on offer and there is an excellent wine list. The extensive menu ranges from ploughman's with home-made bread, a wide choice of cheeses, pickles and chutneys to dishes such as smoked duck with feta cheese and rosemary and plaice fillet with mussels and prawns.

Opening times are 11 am to 3 pm and 6 pm to 11 pm and meals are served from 12 noon to 2.30 pm and from 7 pm to 9.30 pm on Monday to Saturday, from 12 noon to 2.30 pm and from 7 pm to 9 pm on Sunday. Families are welcome and the Compasses also offers accommodation. Telephone: 01725 518231.

The Walk

① With your back to the frontage of the Compasses turn left along the road and follow the gravel path to cross a bridge over the Allen. Continue beside the road and

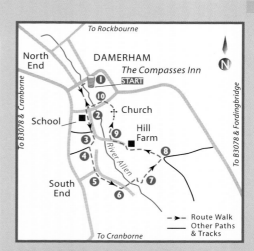

just past the High Street on the right, turn left, following a footpath sign. This leads past gardens and paddocks to take you through a small gate to a quiet lane. The village school, surrounded by woods and meadows, is on your right.

② Follow the lane ahead past a 'No Through Road' sign. Ignore the first footpath sign indicating a path on the right by South View. Shortly afterwards the lane curves left.

③ You will see a footpath sign on the left indicating another path on the right. Turn right as indicated along a narrow hedged path leading past some thatched cottages and gardens.

④ Take the left-hand of the two paths ahead. The path runs through a surprisingly remote wilderness of tangled plants and trees to a stile. Cross this and keep ahead up the path to meet a lane.

⑤ Bear left down the lane past attractive houses. When you come to a three-way finger post keep straight on along the

Damerham's watery world.

gravel track for about 100 yards to a stile and sign on the left just before the entrance to Damerham Trout Lakes.

⑥ Turn left to follow boardwalks and cross bridges over marshes and streams. Go over a stile and keep to the narrow path as it curves left and leads you over another stile. You emerge from this watery world at the foot of a field. Turn right for about 100 yards to cross a low embankment.

⑦ Turn immediately left (unsigned) to walk uphill between the fields to meet a wide hedged crosstrack.

PLACES OF INTEREST NEARBY
About 5 miles north-west of Damerham is **Martin Down Nature Reserve**, 900 acres of unploughed downland, famous for its plants and wildlife.

⑧ Bear left and follow the track for over $^1/_3$ mile through a gate and continue through another gate by Hill Farm to a lane. Turn left along the lane.

⑨ Leave the lane as it curves left in front of a thatched cottage and take the footpath on the right which leads uphill through the churchyard to the south porch of the Norman church of St George, well worth a visit. Follow the gravel path round the tower to leave the churchyard and come to a lane.

⑩ Turn left down the lane to cross the valley and meet our earlier path in front of the school. Turn right through the gate and retrace your steps to the Compasses Inn.

Breamore
The Bat and Ball

MAP: OS OUTDOOR LEISURE 22 (GR 159179)   **WALK 3**   **DISTANCE:** 2 MILES

DIRECTIONS TO START: BREAMORE IS ABOUT 3 MILES NORTH OF FORDINGBRIDGE BESIDE THE A338. THE INN FACES THE ROAD. **PARKING:** PATRONS MAY LEAVE THEIR CARS IN THE INN'S CAR PARK WHILE THEY WALK – PLEASE ASK FIRST.

Breamore lies in the wide valley of the Avon. To the east are the tree-clad slopes of the New Forest and to the west rolling chalk downland. The village is famous for its Elizabethan manor and Saxon church but there is much more to enjoy. The route leads away from the main road, to explore the earlier village, still medieval in appearance. Thatched, half-timbered cottages, many dating from the 17th century, surround a large common, known as the Marsh. Tenants of the Lord of the Manor have had the right to pasture animals there for centuries. A track, a former village 'street', leads to the church and manor and quiet lanes and footpaths cross the Marsh to return to the Bat and Ball Inn, our starting point.

The Bat and Ball

The Bat and Ball is a friendly, welcoming hostelry dating back 250 years. It takes its name from the game of cricket which even at that early date was being played on the Marsh. The inn sign showing an early cricketer with an odd-shaped bat is based on a painting in Breamore House and the distinctive frontage of the inn, with its mullioned windows and Dutch gables, is inspired by the great house. Traditionally, the Bat and Ball is a fishermen's inn as it owns a mile of private fishing along the bank of the river Avon. This facility is free for residents.

Beers include Ringwood Best and Directors and in addition to Dry Blackthorn cider the inn offers a locally produced cider from the Nadder valley. A selection of wines is also available. All the food is freshly prepared. From the wide variety of tempting starters you might choose wild mushroom risotto with parmesan or a bowl of delicious home-made soup. Your main dish might be stir-fried sesame chicken or black marlin supreme cajun style.

Children and dogs are welcome. Opening times on Monday to Saturday are 11 am to 3 pm and 6 pm to 11 pm and meals are served from 12 noon to 2.30 pm and 6 pm to 9 pm. On Sunday the pub is open from 12 noon to 3 pm and food is served from 12 noon to 2.30 pm. In winter, the pub is closed on Sunday evenings. The inn offers accommodation and there is an attractive garden. Telephone: 01725 512252.

The Walk

① Leaving the front of the inn on your right walk through the village. Turn left just past the post office, following the sign for Breamore House, and walk up the lane round the edge of the Marsh to a fork. Take the lane on the right signed for Breamore House, passing a Victorian Lodge on the left. The lane runs uphill to a crossroads. Go straight over and follow the sign for the church. This pleasant lane leads to a gravel crossing track. Ahead, two stone lions guard the entrance to Breamore House. If you wish to visit the house follow the drive and the house is on your right, splendidly situated on a wooded hillside. Retrace your steps down the drive and turn left.

② If you did not visit Breamore House turn right, leaving the entrance to the drive on your left, to walk to the church which has the typical tall Saxon nave, 'long and short' stonework and deep-splayed round-topped windows. The arch leading into the south transept is inscribed with an Anglo-Saxon text which translates as 'Here is

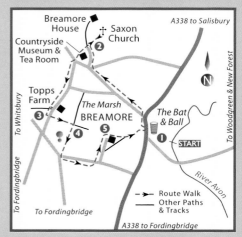

A thatched cottage in Breamore.

made plain the covenant to thee'.

Retrace your steps, following the gravel track past the entrance to Breamore House. Now keep straight on, following the sign for the Countryside Museum and Tea Bar. Pass these on your left and follow the track as it curves left between two half-timbered cottages to a lane. Keep ahead along the lane for about ¹/₂ mile. Pass Topps Farm on your left.

③ About 200 yards beyond the farm turn left over a stile by a footpath sign. Follow the path to the left of a house and head straight across a large field. Over a stile you come to crossing footpaths.

④ Turn right along a grassy path that winds through woods to a lane. Bear left down the lane to a joining lane on the left. Turn left along this quiet way and go through a gate to a gravel track beside the Marsh.

⑤ Turn right past some cottages and continue to a crossing track. Bear left over the Marsh to join a lane which curves left past the back of the school to bring you to the A338 almost opposite the Bat and Ball.

PLACES OF INTEREST NEARBY

Breamore House was completed in 1583 by William Dodington, auditor of the Tower Mint. Later the house passed to Sir Edward Hulse and it is still the Hulse family home. Opening times vary. Telephone: 01725 512468 or 512233.

The Countryside Museum depicts village life in Victorian days with full size replicas of homes and workplaces. For opening times telephone: 01725 512468.

Frogham
The Forester's Arms

MAP: OS OUTDOOR LEISURE 22 (GR 174129) — **WALK 4** — **DISTANCE:** 3 MILES

DIRECTIONS TO START: ONE MILE EAST OF FORDINGBRIDGE, TURN FOR BLISSFORD OFF THE B3078. AT THE Y-JUNCTION BEAR RIGHT FOR FROGHAM AND AT THE NEXT CROSSROAD TURN LEFT FOR BLISSFORD HILL. THE FORESTER'S ARMS IS A FEW YARDS FURTHER ON THE LEFT. **PARKING:** IN THE PUB CAR PARK, WITH PERMISSION.

This walk reveals some of the New Forest's wildest and most remote scenery. Sparkling streams run across the northern Forest, south-west to meet the Avon, carving shallow valleys through the moorland. One of the loveliest is the valley of the Latchmore Brook. The walk follows the brook along the valley as it meanders between the green Forest lawns cropped short by ponies. Wetter patches are rich in wild flowers including the golden spikes of bog asphodel, marsh orchids and insect-catching sundews. A woodland path through the trees of Alderhill Inclosure leads to open moorland which rises to Hampton Ridge offering splendid views south and west as far as the Wiltshire Downs and the Purbeck hills. The route follows the ridge to return to our starting point, the Forester's Arms, in Frogham.

The Forester's Arms

A homely, cottage-style pub, the Forester's Arms offers a warm welcome to everyone. There is no need to worry if you arrive with muddy boots or a dog who has just enjoyed a refreshing swim in the brook. Sensible flagged floors and comfortable wooden settles await you. Doors from the wood-panelled dining room, which is separate from the bar area, lead to a pretty garden with tables and umbrellas in summer, or you can enjoy your drink in the shade of an attractive loggia.

Real ales are JCB, 6X, Malt and Hops, and IPA. Strongbow cider is available and there is a selection of wines. The menu offers a wide choice of dishes from bar snacks to the chef's pies of the day – when we called there was lamb and apricot or turkey and mushroom – and sweets such as pears poached in red wine with chocolate sauce.

Children are welcome and there is a safe playground for them. The pub is open on Monday to Saturday from 11 am to 3 pm and from 6 pm to 11 pm. Food is served Mondays to Thursdays from 12 noon to 2.30 pm and from 6 pm to 9 pm. (Fridays and Saturdays until 9.30 pm.) Sunday opening hours are from 12 noon to 3 pm and from 7 pm to 10.30 pm. Food is available from 12 noon to 2.30 pm but not in the evenings.

There is a large car park and patrons are welcome to leave their cars while they walk provided the management are informed. Telephone: 01425 652294.

The Walk

① With your back to the frontage of the

PLACES OF INTEREST NEARBY
Breamore House is off the A338 to the north (see also Walk 3). Opening times vary. Telephone: 01725 512468 or 512233.

pub turn left to walk along the lane. As the lane dips towards a sharp left-hand bend you will see Abbots Well on your right. This open well is still popular with the Forest animals. The well with a hinged lid beside it was for people. It is recorded as far back as the 13th century when it was called 'Alleyenewell'. When you reach the corner, turn right along a gravel track, (the 'no public access' sign applies to cars only). Follow the track downhill and cross the wooden footbridge a little to the right of the ford over the Latchmore Brook. Return to the gravel track. Ogdens car park is on your left.

② Turn left to cross the car park and take the valley path beside the brook. The path is indistinct at times but just walk along the valley, keeping the brook on your left. The distance to the brook will vary between 50 to 200 yards but you will seldom lose sight of the water. The soft green turf provides pasture for many Forest animals. You will notice a large, worn area known in the Forest as a 'shade'. In spite of its name, a 'shade' is a favoured spot in the open where cool breezes help to disperse the flies which torment animals in hot weather. It is hard to imagine that this tranquil path was once a busy trading route! But in Roman times the path led to potteries in Sloden Wood and the New Forest ware was brought along it to be exported from Hengistbury Head. The remains of kilns and pottery shards can still be found.

③ In a little over a mile you come to the

The valley of the Latchmore Brook.

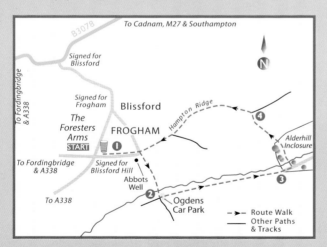

Follow the track which winds up the side of the moor to the top of Hampton Ridge.

④ When you meet a wide gravel crosstrack turn left to follow the ridge with hillsides sloping down to the valley of the Latchmore Brook on your left. During the 18th and early 19th centuries smuggled goods from France were landed at Poole and brought this way to be distributed from Bramshaw Telegraph Station on the Fordingbridge road. Keep to the main track, past a marked cycle route on the left, to meet the lane in Frogham near Abbots Well and rejoin your earlier route. Retrace your steps along the lane to the Forester's Arms.

corner of Alderhill Inclosure. Continue with the Inclosure fence on your left for about 100 yards to a small wooden gate on your left. Turn left through the gate and follow the woodland path ahead. Cross the ford over the Latchmore Brook and leave the wood through another wooden gate.

Fritham
The Royal Oak

| **MAP:** OS OUTDOOR LEISURE 22 (GR 233142) | **WALK 5** | **DISTANCE:** 2½ MILES |

DIRECTIONS TO START: TURN OFF THE B3078 SOUTHAMPTON-FORDINGBRIDGE ROAD 1½ MILES WEST OF THE BELL INN AT BROOK. THEN, TURN RIGHT, SIGNED 'FRITHAM'. THE ROYAL OAK IS ON THE RIGHT. **PARKING:** CONTINUE A LITTLE FURTHER TO TURN LEFT INTO THE PUBLIC CAR PARK.

When the New Forest was declared a royal hunting reserve by William the Conqueror in 1079 its Saxon residents were reluctant to give up their livelihood. Gradually they regained their Forest rights to pasture their animals, gather fuel and improve their land. Small communities formed deep in the heart of the Forest. This walk explores the countryside around Fritham, one of the most remote and fascinating of these settlements. From the pub, the Royal Oak, a lane leads down to Eyeworth pond, a large lake carpeted with white waterlilies and fringed with trees. Today this is an idyllic scene but during the 19th century the valley was the centre of a thriving industry! Schultze gunpowder works, making powder for sporting guns, was established here and the stream was dammed to provide water for cooling purposes. The factory closed in 1910 when the Schultze undertaking became a part of the Nobel Combine and its operations transferred to Scotland. The route follows tracks along the now peaceful valley then rises to cross open moorland before returning to Fritham through old oak and beech woods.

The Royal Oak

This is just the kind of pub you would expect to find in such surroundings. It is a genuine old-fashioned Forest pub, tiny, deep-thatched, with an enormous open fireplace where hams once hung to smoke. Here you can step back in time and enjoy the atmosphere of the real Forest, tranquil and unhurried. The pub is beautifully cared-for by a local family and the oak bar and fittings were made by local craftsmen. From a little bay window you look out over green Forest lawns and grazing ponies. And, as you would expect, the pub is dogs and muddy boots friendly.

Ringwood ales are on offer and there is a selection of excellent quality wines. Home-made soups and ploughman's lunches are available and evening meals by arrangement. The snug, beamed sitting room is ideal for small family get-togethers and parties. There is a large garden shaded by Forest trees. Opening times are 11 am to 3 pm and 6 pm to 11 pm on Monday to Friday; all day on Fridays in summer. Food is served from 12 noon to 3 pm. On Saturdays and Sundays the pub is open throughout the day. Telephone: 023 8081 2606.

The Walk

① From the parking area return to the metalled lane. The Royal Oak is a short distance along the lane to your right. On the corner on your left you will see the black iron postbox placed here to save the postman the walk to the factory. Turn left to walk down the lane to Eyeworth pond. But where is Eyeworth? In the Domesday Book there is a reference to 'Ivare', the

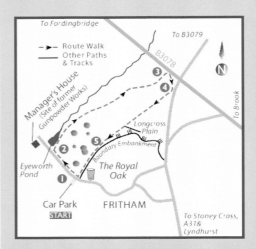

'village under a hill', and it is possible that it was one of the villages that William the Conqueror is alleged to have destroyed when he reserved the area for the royal hunt.

② Turn right to walk beside the lake – too lovely to be called a pond! – with the water on your left. Continue past the Forestry Commission barrier to walk through woodland. After about 200 yards look for the wooden palings surrounding Irons Well on the left. This chalybeate spring was considered beneficial for sore eyes. Follow the embanked track to leave the wood and cross open moorland to a Forestry Commission barrier in front of the main road, the B3078.

③ Before the barrier, turn right along a narrow path that bears away from the main road, which is on your left, to meet a minor road by a traffic sign.

④ Before the minor road, bear right along a wide grassy path between the heather. You will see it more distinctly a short distance ahead. The path curves away from

Eyeworth pond.

the road to run over Longcross Plain, a glorious sight in late summer when the heather is in bloom. Follow the path towards woodland. As you enter the woods you will see a boundary embankment and a

PLACES OF INTEREST NEARBY
New Forest Museum and Visitor Centre in Lyndhurst. Open daily, winter 10 am to 5 pm, from Easter 10 am to 6 pm, August 10 am to 7 pm. Telephone: 023 8028 3914.

fence a few yards away through the trees on your left.

⑤ Bear left to the embankment to join the track running beside it. Follow this track with the embankment on your left round the edge of the fields surrounding Fritham. It is interesting to compare this pastoral landscape with the leafy Forest glades on your right. The track leads directly to the Royal Oak on your left and your car.

Brook
The Green Dragon

DIRECTIONS TO START: BROOK IS ABOUT 1½ MILES WEST OF THE CADNAM ROUNDABOUT ON THE B3079 JUST EAST OF THE JUNCTION WITH THE B3078 (FORDINGBRIDGE) ROAD. **PARKING:** IN THE PUB CAR PARK, WITH PERMISSION.

Some of the New Forest's fascinating history comes alive as you follow this short ramble from Brook, an attractive hamlet of mainly thatched houses set among colourful gardens. From the Green Dragon pub the route follows a quiet lane through woods and over streams. The lane becomes gravelled as it enters a wide glade and leads to the tiny settlement of Canterton, completely surrounded by Forest lawns and trees. From Canterton, a sunken track leads through the woods of Piper's Copse to run past fields and meet a tree-shaded road. If you wish you could make a detour at this point (½ mile each way) to see the Rufus Stone which is reputed to mark the spot where William Rufus was shot through the heart by an arrow while hunting deer one August evening in 1100. The walk follows the road back to Brook.

The Green Dragon

This 15th century thatched inn has low beamed ceilings and enormous fireplaces. Originally it was premises for a wheelwright and coffin-maker and a tile with a crucifix marks the entrance to the former mortuary – now an atttractive family room. It became a beer house 200 years ago. The name of the pub is linked to an intriguing Forest story. According to a document of uncertain date in Berkeley Castle, a 'devouring dragon' once set up home on Burley Hill, in the south of the Forest. Sir Morris Berkeley killed the dragon, to the relief of all. In addition to other properties, Sir Morris owned the manor of Brook so this noble deed has not been forgotten!

Among the many Forest mementos decorating the pub are several 'bends' of leather. These are leather sheets bearing the imprints of the brands used to distinguish livestock pastured on the Forest by owners with Commoner's Rights.

Delicious home-cooked snacks and full meals are available including 'Dragon Platters', platefuls of cheese, ham. pâté or fish served with salad, coleslaw, sweet pickle and crusty rolls. Real ales include London Pride and Ringwood Best. A selection of wines and Inch's Premium cider are also on offer.

Families are welcome and there is a large garden. Opening times during the week are from 11 am to 3 pm and 5 pm to 11 pm. The pub is open all day on Saturdays and Sundays. Food is served from 12 noon to 2 pm and from 6 pm to 9 pm. The management are happy for patrons to leave cars while they walk, (but not before 9 am) provided they have a word with them first. Telephone: 023 8081 3359.

The Walk

① With your back to the frontage of the Green Dragon, turn right to cross a wooden footbridge. Follow the path beside the road past a private lane on your right for Canterton Manor. A few yards further on you come to Canterton Lane on the right.

② Turn right to follow this pleasant lane past houses then downhill to cross a bridge and continue through woods. You pass a prominent white house on the left then the first houses of Canterton village on your right. The name gives a clue to the ancient origins of this tiny place. Canterton means 'the village of the Kentish men'. After the Romans left Britain, Jutish tribes were the first to settle in Kent and the New Forest. Before William the Conqueror's annexation of the Forest earned it its present name, it was called 'Ytene', the land of the Jutes.

Follow the gravel track past the houses for about 50 yards then turn right along a wide green which runs downhill to cross a stream and enter Piper's Copse. The sunken track through the copse can be

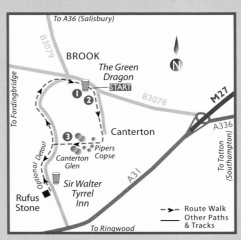

HERE STOOD
THE OAK TREE.
ON WHICH AN ARROW
SHOT BY
SIR WALTER TYRRELL
AT A STAG
GLANCED AND STRUCK
KING WILLIAM
THE SECOND.
SURNAMED RUFUS.
ON THE BREAST,
OF WHICH HE
INSTANTLY DIED.
ON THE SECOND
DAY OF AUGUST.
ANNO 1100.

The Rufus Stone.

muddy. If so, you will find a dry path along the top of the bank to the right of the track. In spring the wood is a mass of bluebells.

③ The bridleway leaves the wood, becomes a narrow lane and brings you to a road. If you would like to see the Rufus Stone turn left and follow the road for about ¹/₂ mile. The famous Stone (now encased in iron) stands on the right just past the Sir Walter Tyrrell Inn. Mystery still surrounds the death of William Rufus. Was his death really an accident or was the arrow fired by a dispossessed Saxon, or perhaps a servant following the orders of his jealous brother Henry? Retrace your steps to the junction with the lane and follow the road back to the B3079 in Brook.

If you do not want to visit the Stone, turn right when you leave the lane to follow the road back to Brook. When you come to the B3079 turn right to walk the few yards back to the Green Dragon.

PLACES OF INTEREST NEARBY
Furzey Gardens, to the south, noted for massed banks of azaleas at their best in May and June. Open daily, 10 am to 5 pm (dusk in winter). Telephone: 023 8081 2464.

Lockerley
The King's Arms

MAP: OS PATHFINDER 1263 (GR 301261)   **WALK 7**   **DISTANCE:** 3 MILES

DIRECTIONS TO START: LOCKERLEY IS ABOUT 6 MILES NORTH-WEST OF ROMSEY. FROM ROMSEY HEAD NORTH ON THE A3057 IN THE DIRECTION OF STOCKBRIDGE. TURN LEFT ALONG THE B3084, SIGNED 'AWBRIDGE', THEN LEFT AGAIN. CONTINUE THROUGH AWBRIDGE TO REACH LOCKERLEY. THE KING'S ARMS IS ON YOUR RIGHT. **PARKING:** PATRONS MAY LEAVE THEIR CARS IN THE PUB CAR PARK WHILE THEY WALK.

Lockerley is a peaceful village set around wide grassy lawns in the valley of the river Dun, a tributary of the Test. It is surrounded by countryside that can only be described as typically English, rolling downs, flower-filled meadows and ancient woodlands. This walk crosses the Dun to take mainly field and woodland paths to the attractive hamlet of Lockerley Green before returning over the fields to the village.

The King's Arms

Our starting point is a genuine village pub where you can be certain of a friendly welcome, excellent ales and good food. The building is over 200 years old and has a wealth of beams and cosy corners decorated with horse brasses. I was told that according to local tradition the pub is haunted but as no one could tell me they had actually seen anything just what or who you may encounter must remain a mystery!

Among the ales are Ringwood Best, Boddingtons and Flowers. There is a good range of hot and cold bar food and more substantial meals include steak and kidney pie and beef casserole. Strongbow cider is available and wine by the glass. Opening times on weekdays are 12 noon to 3.30 pm and 7 pm to 11 pm. From 1 May to 31 September and weekends the pub is open all day from 12 noon to 11 pm. Lunch is served every day except Monday from 12 noon to 2 pm. There is a large garden with a play area for children. Telephone: 01794 340332.

The Walk

① With your back to the frontage of the pub, turn right and after about 100 yards bear right again to follow a lane to the right of Butts Green. The name is a reminder of the days when practice with the longbow was a compulsory part of the upbringing of every boy.

② Cross the road, bear right for a few yards, then turn left to follow a footpath sign and cross the bridge over the river Dun. The river flows prettily here beneath a canopy of willows. Follow the gravel track

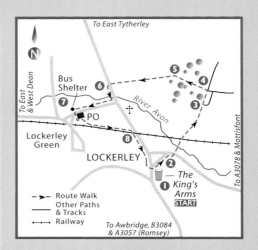

ahead which runs under the railway bridge and becomes a pleasant footpath between hedges. After passing through a small copse, the path turns left towards woodland. Cross a stile into the wood by a National Trust sign.

③ A footpath is indicated turning right, but there is now a right-of-way along the woodland path directly ahead. So follow this path under the trees to a crossing path.

④ Turn left along a beautiful path through the woods. Keep straight on past a path on the right. We came this way in late summer and the path was alive with butterflies. You may see deer as the woods are home to both fallow and roe. Continue past another track on the right and keep ahead over a small wooden bridge to leave the woods.

⑤ Bear half-left to cross a large field. On the other side you come to a wooden stile between wire fences. Cross the stile and bear a little left as you walk down the meadow ahead to cross stiles either side of a bridge. Look right over the fields to see Lockerley Hall. When this was the

The River Dun near Lockerley.

residence of the Dalgety family, waggons used to be sent to fetch the local children for tea and games in the grounds. Continue along a narrow path and through a gate to emerge on the East Tytherley road opposite Above Mill cottages.

⑥ Turn left beside the road to pass Lockerley Water Farm on your left. Cross the bridges over the river Dun and take the next lane on the right, signed for East and West Dean. Follow the lane to Lockerley Green, a

PLACES OF INTEREST NEARBY

Mottisfont Abbey and Gardens (NT), to the east. The gardens are famous for their glorious collection of old roses. From mid to late June the gardens are open daily from 11 am to 8.30 pm and from the end of March to the end of October on Saturday to Wednesday from 12 noon to 6 pm. The house is open from 1 pm to 5 pm on the same days as the garden. Telephone: 01794 340757.

village in its own right with houses grouped around wide expanses of open land, a shop and a post office where you are welcome to enjoy a drink or ice-cream in the garden.

⑦ Opposite the bus shelter, turn left to pass the post office and turn left again down a narrow footpath by a telephone box. The path bears half-right over a field towards a line of trees concealing the railway embankment. As you reach the trees the path curves left along the top of several fields. Over to your left you have a fine view of Lockerley church against a backdrop of woodland.

⑧ Keep straight ahead beside the railway embankment to the East Tytherley road. Turn right towards Lockerley. This part of the road can be busy but after about 100 yards there is a footpath. When you reach Butts Green keep straight ahead, signed for Romsey. The King's Arms is on your left.

Keyhaven
The Gun Inn

MAP: OS OUTDOOR LEISURE 22 (GR 306915)   **WALK 8**   **DISTANCE:** 3½ MILES

DIRECTIONS TO START: THE BEST APPROACH TO KEYHAVEN IS VIA THE A337 LYMINGTON-CHRISTCHURCH ROAD. IN EVERTON TURN FOR MILFORD-ON-SEA ALONG THE B3058. IN MILFORD-ON-SEA TURN LEFT FOR KEYHAVEN. THE GUN IS ON YOUR RIGHT. **PARKING:** PARK IN THE LARGE PUBLIC CAR PARK OPPOSITE THE PUB.

Many areas of Hampshire's coastline have survived the spread of modern development and remain peaceful and remote, rich in birdlife and rare plants. Among them is one of the South's finest nature reserves, a vast expanse of marshland stretching east from Keyhaven to Lymington. The best way to explore the marshes is to follow the sea wall and that is the route I have chosen for this walk. Seaward of the wall huge numbers of birds probe the mud and saltmarsh for worms and shellfish. Inland, brackish lagoons and rough pasture attract more wildlife including the stately heron. And there is history to enjoy too. The production of sea salt was an important industry along this low-lying coast from Roman times until the early 19th century and you can still see the embanked rectangles of the salterns and the mounds which once supported windpumps.

28

The Gun Inn

Our starting point in Keyhaven is the Gun Inn, overlooking the harbour wall. The Gun is a charming cottage-like pub attractively draped with fishing nets and lobster pots. A small cannon is mounted above the porch, not, I must add, to deter customers but to commemorate Colonel Peter Hawker, a noted 19th century wildfowler who lived next door. There is a salty, sea-going atmosphere about this 17th century pub with its barrels and anchors and walls bearing posters requesting crews for men o'war. In the past, smugglers discussed their plans over a mug of good Gun ale and I was told that a secret tunnel runs beneath the bar to the harbour entrance!

Apart from the bar areas there is a special room for families and a delightful beamed 'snug' in what was once a stable. Real ales include Wadworth 6X, Flowers Original, Marston's Pedigree, Strongs Best Bitter and Ringwood Old Thumper. Wines and cider are on offer and a choice of 130 malt whiskeys. Bar snacks include ploughman's and a range of salad platters which, among other tasty treats, offers local dressed crab. For a more substantial meal you might opt for gammon steak and pineapple, chicken tikka masala or supreme of salmon.

There is a garden with a play area for children. Opening times on Monday to Saturday are 11 am to 3 pm and 6 pm to 11 pm; on Sundays 12 noon to 3 pm and 6 pm to 10.30 pm. Meals are served from 12 noon to 2.20 pm and from 6 pm to 9.20 pm. Telephone: 01590 642391.

The Walk

① Leaving the front of the Gun on your left turn right down the lane marked 'No Through Road' which runs beside the harbour wall. Cross the sluice gates over the Avon Water. On the right you enjoy a splendid view over the little harbour, lively with pleasure yachts and fishing boats, to the castle and lighthouse on the end of Hurst Spit and the hills of the Isle of Wight.

② Leave the lane and follow the footpath sign on the right through a gate to follow the gravel track along the sea wall. The track widens to run beside the marshes then rises and narrows as it regains the height of the wall. Have your binoculars ready as you follow the wall through the nature reserve. Among the birds you may expect to see are curlews, dunlins, redshanks, oyster-catchers and Sandwich terns with their striking black and white colouring and graceful swooping flight. After the wall skirts a pool, look inland to see the remains of the salterns. Go through

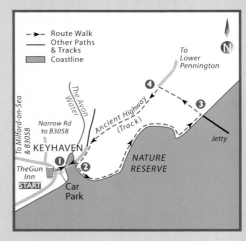

Keyhaven harbour.

a gate and continue along the wall as it bears right then turns sharply left to a jetty.

PLACES OF INTEREST NEARBY
Hurst Castle. A ferry runs from Keyhaven to Hurst Castle daily from May to the end of October, leaving Keyhaven on the hour from 10 am and returning on the half-hour until 5.30 pm. Telephone: 01425 610784. The Castle is open daily from April to September, 10 am to 6 pm; rest of the year at weekends only, 10 am to 4 pm. Telephone: 01590 642344.

③ With the jetty on your right, turn left along a wide track leading inland. Follow this for about ½ mile to go through a gate to a lane.

④ Turn left along a track known as the Ancient Highway. Once this was a road linking Lower Pennington with Keyhaven serving the saltworks and providing a convenient route for smugglers. Go through a gate to a lane and continue past the footpath sign to the sea wall to return to the Gun.

Pilley
The Fleur de Lys

MAP: OS OUTDOOR LEISURE 22 (GR 328983)   **WALK 9**   **DISTANCE:** 2 MILES

DIRECTIONS TO START: PILLEY IS ABOUT 2 MILES NORTH OF LYMINGTON. TURN FOR BOLDRE OFF THE A337, AND FOLLOW THE MINOR ROAD AS IT BEARS RIGHT THEN LEFT TO PILLEY. THE FLEUR DE LYS IS ON YOUR RIGHT. **PARKING:** PATRONS MAY LEAVE THEIR CARS IN THE PUB CAR PARK WHILE THEY WALK OR PARK IN THE VILLAGE.

A ramble beside the upper reaches of the Lymington river through a stunning nature reserve is the highlight of this walk. Before William Cross built a toll bridge dam with two sluices across the mouth of the river in 1731, the water was tidal and formed a wide valley. Now the river flows lazily along the valley through a jungle of reed-beds and grassland home to a variety of wildlife including herons, kingfishers and otters. The walk begins at the Fleur de Lys pub in Pilley, a small village close to the east bank of the river. Footpaths and lanes lead past 'Gilpins', once the residence of the 18th century author William Gilpin. After following the riverside we return to Pilley up an ancient sunken track.

The Fleur de Lys

Long, low and thatched with half-timbered whitewashed walls, the Fleur de Lys is a fascinating pub. Originally the building was a pair of forester's cottages and became an inn as far back as 1096! Tree roots and a fireplace opening can still be seen beside the narrow stone-flagged entrance hall. The two cosy bars are named after characters in Captain Marryat's *Children of the New Forest*, Jacob Armitage and Beverley of Arnwood. As is only proper, this venerable building is haunted by two ghosts!

The choice of beers includes Flowers Original, Morland Old Speckled Hen, Marston's Pedigree, Wadworth 6X and locally brewed Ringwood Best. Cider is Scrumpy Jack and there is a carefully selected wine list. The extensive menu offers tempting starters – you might try Giant Woodland Mushrooms filled with garlic butter, followed by imaginatively cooked main dishes such as Thatch Pie, beef steak in rich gravy laced with port. Sweets include a delicious fresh fruit pavlova.

Families are welcome and there is an attractive garden with a 14th century wishing well – make a wish, toss in a coin and contribute to the restoration of Boldre's historic church. Dogs are welcome. Opening times on Monday to Saturday are 11.30 am to 3 pm and 6 pm to 10.30 pm (11 pm Friday and Saturday). On Sunday the pub is open from 12 noon to 3.30 pm and from 7 pm to 10.30 pm. Meals are served from 12 noon to 2 pm (2.30 pm on Saturday and Sunday) and from 6 pm (7 pm Sunday) to 9.30 pm. Overnight accommodation is also available. Telephone: 01590 672158.

The Walk

NB: It is advisable to wear wellies, boots or strong shoes for this walk.

① Turn left from the car park entrance, then left again following the footpath sign to follow a grassy path and cross a stile. Keep ahead beside a meadow with a hedge on your left. Originally the land around Pilley was given by William the Conqueror to William de Redvers. Later it was inherited by a kinsman, William de Vernun, a supporter of the Dauphin of France. William's coat of arms included the Fleur de Lys which accounts for an English country pub having a French name!

② Cross another stile to a lane and turn right. Continue to a T-junction and turn left to Vicar's Hill. The lane bears left past the entrance to Southlands School. The fine Georgian House ahead is Gilpins. Presented to the living of Boldre and Pilley in 1777, William Gilpin spent much time exploring the New Forest. His book *Remarks on Forest Scenery* and his views on the 'picturesque' greatly influenced contemporary attitudes towards nature.

The Lymington Reedbeds Nature Reserve.

③ Bear right to leave Gilpins on your left and follow the lane as it descends into the Lymington river valley.

④ About 300 yards after a sharp right hand bend, look for a footpath sign on the right. Turn right to enter the Lymington Reedbeds Nature Reserve and follow the footpath beneath the trees. After going through a gate the path runs closer to the river. Willows trail loose branches in the water and where the reeds give way to

grassland the river banks are brilliant in summer with tall stands of pink and white comfrey and spikes of purple loosestrife.

NB: If the path by the river is muddy, pick your way to a drier path running parallel on the left closer to the river.

⑤ After almost a mile alongside the river go through a gate to a sunken lane. Bear right up the lane. At the T-junction turn right along the verge. Just past the entrance to the vicarage take the footpath on the left which runs parallel with the road past the William Gilpin Primary School. School Lane on your right leads to Spinners Gardens. The Fleur de Lys is a short distance ahead on your right.

PLACES OF INTEREST NEARBY
Spinners is a superb woodland garden. Open daily except Monday, 10 am to 5 pm, from late April to August. Telephone: 01590 673347.

Wherwell
The White Lion

MAP: OS PATHFINDERS 1242 AND 1222 (GR 389409)

WALK 10

DISTANCE: 2½ MILES

DIRECTIONS TO START: WHERWELL LIES ON THE B3420 ABOUT 4 MILES SOUTH OF ANDOVER. DRIVE INTO THE VILLAGE AND TAKE THE TURNING BY THE WAR MEMORIAL (A TALL COLUMN) DOWN CHURCH STREET. **PARKING:** CAR PARK OFF CHURCH STREET, ON THE LEFT JUST BEFORE THE CHURCHYARD GATES.

Wherwell, nestling beside Hampshire's famous trout stream, the Test, is an enchanting village of deep-thatched houses and cottages, many half-timbered and colourwashed white or pink. On the other side of the river, across a common famous for its wildlife, lies another attractive village, Chilbolton. On this walk we visit both villages and explore the beautiful countryside which surrounds them.

The White Lion

This former coaching inn has welcomed travellers and locals alike since 1611. We have enjoyed its friendly atmosphere on several occasions and can vouch for the truth of the statement on its card: 'The White Lion welcomes the Spring – and Ramblers all the year round!' Lunchtime and dinner menus vary, but a wide choice includes mouthwatering steak and fish dishes and a very tempting lasagne.

Beers on offer include Flowers Original and Boddingtons. Strongbow cider is available and a selection of wines. Opening times on Monday to Saturday are from 10 am to 2.30 pm (until 3 pm Saturday) and in the evening from 6 pm to 11 pm on Wednesday to Saturday and from 7 pm on Monday and Tuesday. Sunday times are from 12 noon to 3 pm and 7 pm to 10.30 pm. Meals are served from 12 noon to 2 pm and from 7 pm to 9.30 pm except on Sunday evenings. Overnight accommodation is available. Telephone: 01264 860317.

Patrons may leave their cars in the car park while they walk (ask permission first) but the inn is popular and it is better to use the car park in Church Street a short distance away. This also gives you the opportunity to see a particularly charming and historic part of the village.

The Walk

① Turn left from the car park entrance through the churchyard. The church was rebuilt in the mid-19th century but medieval survivals include an effigy of a remarkable woman, the Blessed Euphemia. From 1226 to 1257 she ruled the abbey founded here at the end of the 10th century

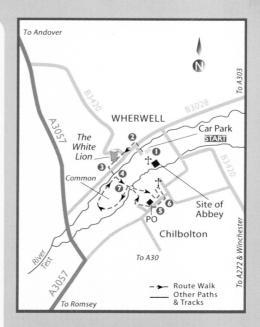

by Queen Elfrida. To see the site of the abbey cross the grass to the right of the church porch and look over the churchyard wall. The large 19th century house replaced an earlier house built here after the abbey was dissolved in 1540.

Retrace your steps through the churchyard gate and walk up picturesque Church Street.

② Turn left to walk through the village and continue straight ahead at the crossroads past the White Lion car park along the Stockbridge road for about ¼ mile.

③ Take the bridleway on the left, signed 'Test Way' to cross the wooden footbridges over the river.

④ Follow the gravelled path over Chilbolton Common to cross a bridge over a stream. Continue for about 50 yards to a

The village of Wherwell.

post marked with footpath signs in front of a parking area. Just before the post turn left along a narrow path which leads over a gravel track past power lines. Keep straight on past a path on the left. Our path curves right over a small bridge. Cross the stile and the grass ahead with trees close on your right to follow a gravel path which meets the road in Chilbolton opposite the Abbot's Mitre pub.

⑤ Turn left and continue through the village to a footpath sign on the left. Take this for a few yards, then turn right through an iron gate. Cross a field, go through a gate and turn right through the gate into the churchyard of St Mary the Less. The church dates from the 13th century and

well repays a visit. From the south porch follow the path directly ahead to emerge in the village street.

⑥ Turn right to walk through the village. A few yards past the thatched post office turn right, following a footpath sign. The path bears left to a lane. Turn right to the Common. Follow the gravel track leading right then curving left towards the parking area. About 30 yards before the parking area take the path on the left to rejoin your earlier route by the post marked with footpath signs. Bear left to retrace your steps over the stream.

⑦ Turn immediately left to head east over the Common towards a fringe of trees. Keep to the main path which swings right as it comes to the trees. Soon you will see the Test on your left. Follow the path to rejoin your earlier route by the Test bridges. Turn left to retrace your steps over the bridges then right through the village to your car.

PLACES OF INTEREST NEARBY

Andover Museum, the Museum of the Iron Age is based on the finds made at Danebury Ring. Open all year on Tuesday to Saturday from 10 am to 5 pm; from April to September also on Sundays, 2 pm to 5 pm. Telephone: 01264 366283.

Longparish
The Plough Inn

MAP: OS PATHFINDER 1223 (GR 427442)   **WALK 11**   **DISTANCE:** 2 MILES

DIRECTIONS TO START: LONGPARISH IS ABOUT 5 MILES EAST OF ANDOVER. TURN NORTH OFF THE A303 FOR LONGPARISH ALONG THE B3048. **PARKING:** AFTER ABOUT A MILE, OPPOSITE A LANE ON THE LEFT, LOOK CAREFULLY FOR A SIGN MARKED 'VILLAGE HALL CAR PARK' ON THE RIGHT AND FOLLOW THE SIGN TO PARK UNDER THE TREES. ALTERNATIVELY PATRONS MAY LEAVE CARS IN THE PLOUGH INN CAR PARK ABOUT ¼ MILE FURTHER UP THE ROAD.

This walk in the rolling countryside of the Upper Test valley starts from a village that lives up to its name. The houses and cottages, many attractively half-timbered and thatched, stretch for more than two miles beside the river, forming several small hamlets. For this walk I have chosen Middleton. Here the Test flows serenely through the meadows past a 12th century church and paths through cornfields lead to the ancient oak woods of Harewood Forest. Our starting point is the public car park near the Plough Inn.

The Plough Inn

A traditional, family-run inn, the Plough has a cosy, welcoming atmosphere. Wooden arches divide the spacious interior so you can always find a quiet table and comfortably padded window-seats will tempt you to linger.

A varied range of real ales plus the inn's very own 'Furrowed Firkin' is on offer. Dry Blackthorn cider is available and there is an extensive wine list. The menu offers something to please everybody from a range of sandwiches – the 'Triple Decker' consists of three slices of granary bread with crab and prawns – to substantial home-made pies. Fish and game dishes are a speciality.

Opening times on Monday to Saturday are 11 am to 3 pm and 6 pm to 11 pm. On Sunday the Plough opens from 12 noon to 3 pm and 7 pm to 11 pm. Food is served from 12 noon to 2.30 pm and from 6.30 pm to 9.30 pm, 7 pm to 9 pm on Sunday evening.

The inn's superb garden has won the Test Valley in Bloom award more than once. Telephone: 01264 720358.

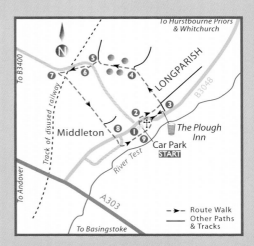

The Walk

① Return to the road along a small path between two black posts opposite a 'School' sign. Turn right past the village hall on your left.

② The main road begins to curve right. Do not follow it but keep straight on down an asphalted lane signed for Greenholme and Greenacre. Go through a gate and after a few yards follow the narrow path ahead to the sports field. Continue beside the field with trees on your right then bear left round the edge of the field to a wooden door in the hedge with signs for the Test Way. Through the door a path leads you past cottages to a lane.

③ Turn left past a footpath on the right. After about 50 yards the lane becomes a grassy track. Follow this pleasant way shaded by trees on your left with views over curving fields dotted with small woods on your right. After about ½ mile you come to a crosstrack.

④ Turn left. The track climbs to enter part of Harewood Forest. Follow the woodland track for about ¼ mile. Now for some careful navigation!

⑤ Opposite joining tracks on the right and left look for double iron gates across the grass on the left. Turn left go through a gap beside the gates or cross by a stile a few yards to your right. Keep ahead to a lane.

⑥ Turn right along the lane which soon leads you across the bridge over a disused railway. The lane descends and you will see

Longparish village stocks beside the churchyard wall.

a footpath sign on the left.

⑦ Turn left and follow a woodland path that dips over the disused track and continues through the trees. As you emerge from the wood the path curves a little left beside fields with a tall hedge dotted with trees on your left. Continue for about ³/₄ mile. When the path curves left keep straight on, still with a hedge on your left.

⑧ Go through a gate and cross the B3048 to walk down the lane ahead. Before the

PLACES OF INTEREST NEARBY
Whitchurch Silk Mill, to the north-east: 200 years of history and still powered by water. Open all year, every day except Mondays, 10.30 am to 5 pm. Telephone: 01256 892065 (customer enquiries), 893882 (for bookings).

lane bends right turn left through a small gate. Take the path over the field with the Test half-buried in rushes on your right. Soon the river runs more freely and becomes part of a scene worthy of Constable – a thatched house and barns overlooked by the chequered stone and flint tower of the parish church.

⑨ Go through a gate, pass the barn and turn through a small gate on the left to cross the churchyard. The church contains a great deal of interest including a beautiful East window designed by Edward Burne-Jones and part of an ancient rood screen fastened to the lid of the font. Turn left from the church porch to leave by the main gate. On the left you will see the village stocks. Continue to the B3048. Turn right to visit the Plough or left to return to the car park.

St Mary Bourne
The Bourne Valley Inn

MAP: OS PATHFINDERS 1223 AND 1203
(GR 426499)

WALK 12

DISTANCE: 2½ MILES

DIRECTIONS TO START: ST MARY BOURNE IS ABOUT 4 MILES NORTH OF ANDOVER BESIDE THE B3048. TURN FOR THE VILLAGE FROM THE A343 AT HURSTBOURNE TARRANT TO REACH THE BOURNE VALLEY INN ON YOUR RIGHT. **PARKING:** PATRONS MAY LEAVE THEIR CARS AT THE INN WHILE THEY WALK – BUT ASK PERMISSION FIRST.

St Mary Bourne is one of the most beautiful of the many delightful villages tucked away in the river valleys in north-west Hampshire. On either side of the Bourne stream which flows through the village, gently curving meadows rise to wooded hillsides. From the village, with its rows of thatched, flint and brick or half-timbered houses, our path crosses meadows and then climbs to the Portway, a Roman road built to link Old Sarum and Silchester. Downland paths with fine views lead to a cobbled byway which brings us back to our starting point, the Bourne Valley Inn.

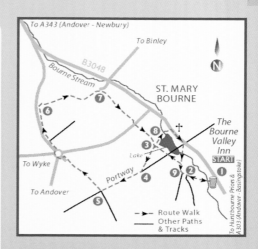

The Bourne Valley Inn

Until the late 18th century this attractive building was ten cottages and the inn retains the quiet charm of a real village home, offering the friendliest of welcomes. It has something for everyone: a cosy bar, excellent hotel accommodation and a spacious restaurant housed in The Barn which is magnificently timbered in green oak.

There is always a choice of three real ales and these vary from month to month. The bar menu offers everything from speciality baguettes – a cold choice might be poached salmon and prawn with Marie Rose sauce – to Bangers and Mash! An equally wide choice awaits you in the restaurant with steak and fish dishes a speciality. There is a patio, a charming streamside garden and an enclosed play area for children. Dogs are welcome.

Opening times are from 11 am to 11 pm from Mondays to Saturdays and from 12 noon to 10.30 pm on Sundays. Food is served from 12 noon to 2 pm and from 7 pm to 9 pm. If you intend a group visit advance booking would be very much appreciated. Telephone: 01264 738361.

The Walk

① With the front of the inn on your left, turn left down the side of the building, leaving the inn sign on your right. Cross the gravel into the streamside garden and turn right to cross the stream over a small white-railed bridge. Follow the path ahead to cross a bridge over the Bourne. Go through a gate and continue over the meadow passing a house on your left to a gate. Go through the gate to a narrow lane.

② Turn right, continue past a lane on the left, and keep to the lane as it curves right. After about 50 yards turn left, directed by a footpath sign. Go through a gate and follow the path ahead with a lake on your right. At the other end of the lake you come to a gate.

③ Do not go through the gate, but turn left through a small gate (lift the latch on the top) and walk up the meadow towards woodland. Go over a stile and keep straight on uphill through the trees to leave the wood. Follow the grassy path ahead to go through a gap in a a thick hedge.

④ At this point you join the Portway. Go straight on with a lower hedge on your left, which bears very slightly left beside the hedge. Continue to a crossing track.

⑤ Turn right and follow the track past a house on the left and farm buildings on the right to a crossroads. Cross over with a signpost on your right, cross the next lane and take the unsigned narrow lane directly ahead. Follow the lane, past a footpath on

The lake at St Mary Bourne.

the right, until, at the foot of a descent, you come to a path on the right signed 'Byway'.

⑥ Turn right along this beautiful raised woodland path and follow it past a path on the left as it descends towards the village and becomes asphalted. Bear right for a few yards to a gate on the right.

⑦ Go through the gate and follow the field path over two stiles. A narrow path beside a hedge on the left leads to a lane. Cross, go through a squeeze stile and continue through a gate to a sports field.

PLACES OF INTEREST NEARBY
Finkley Down Farm Park is open from April (or Easter if earlier) to September, 10.30 am to 6 pm. Café. Telephone: 01264 352195.

Cross the field towards a gate and just before it turn left down the side of the sports field with the lake on your right. Go through a gate, bearing a little right past the entrance to the village hall to the road.

⑧ Bear right over the Bourne and follow the road to the 12th century church which has a huge Tournai marble font. Continue along the road for another 30 yards and turn right along a lane marked 'Private Road' (applies to cars only).

⑨ After about 200 yards the road divides. Follow the left-hand lane to the stile on the left which you crossed earlier in the walk. Retrace your steps to the Bourne Valley Inn and your car.

Micheldever
The Half Moon & Spread Eagle

MAP: OS PATHFINDER 1243 AND 1223 (GR 517389)	WALK 13	DISTANCE: 3½ MILES

DIRECTIONS TO START: THE HALF-MOON AND SPREAD EAGLE IS AT THE SOUTH-EAST END OF MICHELDEVER VILLAGE. HEADING NORTH, TURN OFF THE A33 WINCHESTER-BASINGSTOKE ROAD FOLLOWING THE SIGN FOR MICHELDEVER VILLAGE ONLY. THE PUB IS JUST OVER A MILE FURTHER ON YOUR RIGHT. IF HEADING SOUTH ALONG THE A33, TURN FOR MICHELDEVER, DRIVE INTO THE VILLAGE, THEN TURN LEFT ALONG THE OLD WINCHESTER ROAD TO THE PUB WHICH IS ON YOUR LEFT. **PARKING:** PATRONS ARE WELCOME TO LEAVE CARS IN THE PUB CAR PARK WHILE WALKING.

Micheldever is one of Hampshire's most attractive villages. Set in a peaceful river valley, Micheldever's thatched, half-timbered houses cluster around a network of quiet lanes. It comes as no surprise to read that the village was once owned by King Alfred who had a home there. This walk leaves the village to take woodland and meadow paths to explore the valley of the River Dever.

The Half Moon & Spread Eagle

You would expect a village as charming as Micheldever to have an excellent pub and the Half Moon & Spread Eagle will not disappoint you. No one is quite certain of the age of the pub. Inside, thick walls, deep window seats and heavily beamed ceilings belie the pub's neat, whitewashed exterior. We were told that over the years it has acquired two rather restless ghosts who fortunately confine their activities to the attics! We were curious to find out why the pub had such a long name and evidently at one time there were two pubs in Micheldever – one was the Half Moon and the other the Spread Eagle. One pub burnt down so the other adopted both names.

You can enjoy your drink and meal in the spacious bar or separate restaurant or if you wish you can draw up a comfortable chair in front of the fire. We can thoroughly recommend the delicious food on offer. When we called dishes included brace of whole mackerel baked with tomatoes, garlic and shallots, steak and Guinness pie and honey and mint marinated lamb cutlets with a crème fraiche dressing. Real ales included Ruddles, Abbots, 3X and Caledonian 80 shillings but the choice is varied from time to time. Opening times during the week are from 12 noon to 3 pm and from 6 pm to 11 pm. Sundays the pub is open from 12 noon to 3 pm and from 6 pm to 10.30 pm. Food is served Monday to Thursday from 12 noon to 2 pm and from 6 pm to 9 pm. Fridays and Saturdays from 12 noon to 2 pm and from 6 pm to 9.30 pm. (Sundays 8.30 pm) Telephone: 01962 774339.

The Walk

① Leave the front of the Half Moon & Spread Eagle on your left and walk up the road. Ignore a footpath sign pointing up the bank on the left and continue to a bridleway sign on the left.

② Turn left following the sign along a narrow hedged path which soon becomes more open and grassy and finally asphalted to bring you to a lane.

③ Cross the lane and follow the path ahead which rises and curves left to open fields. Keep ahead between fields to a crosspath. Do not go as far as the line of trees you will see directly ahead of you.

④ At the crosspath turn right. At first you are still walking between open fields but after about 150 yards you reach the westerly end of an avenue of trees. Follow the narow earth path running between the trees. On the other side of the trees, on your left, meadows slope down to the river Dever, hidden in the undergrowth. Continue along the tree-bordered path for about a mile

The path to the Dever Valley near Micheldever

until another avenue of trees threaded by a narrow earth path crosses your way.

⑤ Turn left to follow the narrow path downhill. The path crosses the Dever and to a division just before you come to a boarded fence on the left.

⑥ We turn left here to follow the route of the walk. But if you would like to see the charming little hamlet of West Stratton – more thatched and half-timbered houses – keep straight on with the boarded fence on your left. When you reach the corner of a road turn left to walk up to the village. Then retrace your steps to the division at 6 and turn right. From the division the path runs through a gateway into a meadow. Keep straight ahead over the meadow with a hedge a few yards away on your right. The Dever runs through a shallow channel over the meadow on your right. The wide grassy path continues between high hedges and passes tall trees on the right to a division. Take the left hand path which tunnels under trees then crosses an open area to go

through a gate into another long meadow. Keep ahead with trees close on your right. When you see the houses of Northbrook beyond the meadow ahead, turn left over the grass for a lovely view of the Dever at the point where it broadens to form small lakes.

⑦ Go through a gate and follow the path down the meadow to go through another gate. Follow the narrow hedged path ahead leading to the road in Northbrook opposite the turning for Weston Colley.

⑧ Turn left to cross the bridge over the Dever. Beyond the bridge a footpath sign on the right indicates two paths. Take the left hand path through gates to cross the churchyard. Micheldever church is as attractive as the village, with an unusual Classical style octagon nave. Leave the church on your left and cross the churchyard to the road opposite the school. Turn right to a T-junction. Bear left, then shortly right up Winchester Road to return to your car.

Ecchinswell
The Royal Oak

MAP OS PATHFINDERS 1187 AND 1203 (GR 503606)	WALK 14	DISTANCE: 3 MILES

DIRECTIONS TO START: ECCHINSWELL IS 5 MILES SOUTH OF NEWBURY. TURN SOUTH FOR THE VILLAGE FROM THE A339 NEWBURY-KINGSCLERE ROAD. **PARKING:** PATRONS MAY LEAVE THEIR CARS IN THE PUB CAR PARK WHILE THEY WALK.

Originally Ecchinswell was a scattering of thatched cottages in the shelter of the North Hampshire Downs, grouped around the source of a little stream, the Ecch. Today the village reflects all styles but it is still one of Hampshire's treasures. The Ecch rises in a deep pool then flows beside the road, overlooked by thatched houses and cottages surrounded by beautiful gardens. Walks from the village usually head south to nearby Watership Down, made famous by Richard Adams, but for a change this walk explores the attractive, thickly-wooded country to the north. We start from the Royal Oak pub in the centre of the village.

The Royal Oak

So warm is the welcome that it is impossible not to feel at home in the Royal Oak. The building is very old – possibly late 14th century – and began life as a drover's cottage. Additions over the centuries have created space for everyone to relax in comfort. There is a cosy beamed public bar, a spacious lounge bar and a separate games room. In a building so old you would expect a ghost and I was told that mysterious unexplained tappings are sometimes heard. Evidently this ghost, unlike children, is to be heard but not seen!

The bar menu includes an all-day breakfast and a variety of baguettes. Chicken, bacon and mushroom pie is an example of the more substantial dishes. As all the food is freshly prepared it is a good plan to order your meal beforehand if you intend to eat after your walk. Beers include Greene King, IPA, Spitfire and Flowers Original. Cider is Strongbow and there is a selection of wines. Opening times are perfect for walkers – from 12 noon to 11 pm all the year round. Meals are served from 12 noon to 2.30 pm and from 6.30 pm to 9.15 pm. Dogs and children are very welcome and there is a large tree-shaded garden. Telephone: 01635 298280.

The Walk

① Leaving the front of the pub on your right, walk up the village to the war memorial. Cross the road and turn left over the car park of the village hall. Leave the hall on your left to walk between the hall and a smaller building on your right to the sports field. Bear a little right to continue along the edge of the sports field with a hedge on your right. Keep ahead through a gap in a hedge. Now a wide grassy path leads you into pleasant countryside with the hedge still on your right and enters splendid woodland where you may see deer. You emerge from the trees to continue between hedges and through a small wood to go round a gate to a lane.

② Turn right along the lane for about ¼ mile to a footpath sign on your left which indicates a path on your right. Turn right up a stepped bank and continue along a narrow path with a fence on your right to a field. Turn left to walk beside the field with woods on your left. Follow the path as it continues beside fields to a wide gravelled track.

③ Bear right along the track with woods on your left and views over fields and rolling downland on your right.

④ As you approach houses the track curves right to pass a large metal barn. Leave the track and bear left beside a fence over the grass to a road. Cross the road and

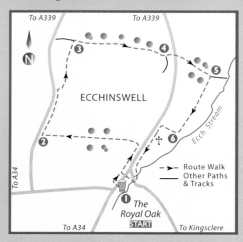

The River Ecch.

take the footpath ahead. This is another beautiful wide woodland way bordered in places in summer by stands of wild angelica over six feet in height!

⑤ After about ¼ mile, just before the track leaves the woods, turn right to follow a path with the edge of the woods close on the left. When you see an iron gate a little to your left, squeeze past a large tree and

PLACES OF INTEREST NEARBY
Sandham Memorial Chapel at Burghclere contains Stanley Spencer's magnificent murals depicting his experiences as a medical orderly during the First World War. Opening times vary; for details telephone: 01635 278394.

cross a stile on the left. Bear right along the edge of a meadow, fence on the right. Cross a stile on the right which leads to a narrow crosspath with a small brick-built pumping station on the left.

⑥ Turn right through a gate and follow a good path straight ahead to a lane. Bear left down the lane past the church towards the Royal Oak. But just before you reach the pub turn left along the road signed for Kingsclere and follow it as it curves right beside the stream to reveal a delightful corner of the village. Before the road curves left, turn right over a bridge, follow the path ahead and turn right when you come to the road to return to the Royal Oak.

Ampfield
The White Horse

MAP: OS PATHFINDERS 1263, 1264 (GR 401232)	WALK 15	DISTANCE: 3½ MILES

DIRECTIONS TO START: AMPFIELD IS BESIDE THE B3090 ROMSEY-WINCHESTER ROAD, ABOUT 4 MILES EAST OF THE CENTRE OF ROMSEY. THE WHITE HORSE IS SET BACK A LITTLE FROM THE ROAD – LOOK FOR THE SIGN. **PARKING:** PATRONS MAY LEAVE THEIR CARS AT THE PUB WHILE THEY WALK BUT ARE ASKED TO PARK AT THE REAR.

All the family will enjoy this woodland walk. The paths are level and easy to follow, and there is a wealth of wildlife to discover. Although Ampfield lies beside a busy road, it is a village of trees still surrounded by part of the great forests that once spread east from the Test valley to the river Itchen. Our route heads north through Ampfield Wood – an attractive mix of oak, beech, yew and sweet chestnut with a sprinkling of pines – to the hamlet of Lower Slackstead, a handful of thatched cottages. Meadow and woodland paths lead back to our starting point, the White Horse.

The White Horse

Travellers between Romsey and Winchester have been welcomed at the White Horse since early in the 17th century. The pub is long and low with white, half-timbered walls, huge inglenook fireplaces and spacious bar and restaurant areas. If the walls could speak they would have many tales to tell. Perhaps they could tell us more about the shadowy caped figure, the most often seen of the pub's several ghosts, and reveal what dramatic events are connected with the priest's hiding hole leading to an escape route under the eaves!

The inn stocks a variety of real ales. Strongbow cider is on offer and there is an interesting selection of wines which you can order by the glass if you wish. A wide range of home-cooked food is available, the most popular dish being a delicious steak and kidney pudding. Examples of other tempting meals are braised beef in shallots and ginger and lamb with port and redcurrant. For a really sinful dessert you could try a White Horse Special, crunchy meringue with butter toffee ice-cream topped with whipped cream and butterscotch sauce.

The pub is open all day from 11 am to 11 pm. (12 noon to 10.30 pm on Sundays) and meals are served from 12 noon to 3 pm and from 6 pm to 9 pm. There is an attractive garden overlooking open countryside. Dogs on leads are welcome in the garden and bar areas. The White Horse does get very busy, so book if you would like Sunday lunch. Telephone: 01794 368356.

The Walk

① With the front of the White Horse on your right follow the footway beside the road past the entrance to the golf club. Continue past the turning to the village hall and turn left, following the sign for Knapp, the oldest part of the village. On the right you pass the war memorial and the little Victorian school built, like so many Victorian buildings, to look as much like a church as possible. Many of the charming houses lining Knapp Lane are 18th century or earlier. Until the 1930s Ampfield was a feudal village, dominated by the owners of Ampfield House. Estate houses feature tile-hung walls and intricately latticed windows.

② At the end of the public lane you come to Ampfield Wood. Turn left past a gate and a Forestry Commission notice along a good track into the wood. The track is called Claypit Road. When the brick-making industry flourished at nearby Chandler's Ford, Ampfield villagers earned a little extra money digging pits and extracting clay to supply the works. Keep

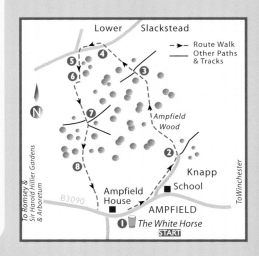

50

PLACES OF INTEREST NEARBY
Sir Harold Hillier Gardens and Arboretum, to the west, near Romsey. Open all year from 10.30 am to 6 pm (or dusk if earlier). Telephone: 01794 368787.

An estate cottage in Knapp Lane.

ahead along the main track over all crossing tracks for about a mile.

③ Keep straight on when the track becomes less wide and grassy to pass a gate. The path continues past Slackstead House to a lane.

④ Turn left along the lane to a bridleway sign on the left opposite a thatched house.

⑤ Bear left as the sign directs through a gate, and over the grass ahead to go through another gate and follow a narrow path with woods on your left and a fence on your right.

⑥ Through the next gate you enter a meadow. Turn right for about 30 yards then turn left as the sign directs to continue beside meadows with a hedge on your right.

⑦ After going through another gate into woods bear left past a track immediately on your right to a Y-junction. Take the right-hand path and follow it past a joining path on the left. Continue straight ahead over a crosstrack to leave the woods through a gate.

⑧ Bear half-left across the meadow to go through a gate to the left of a wood. Follow the path with the wood at first on your right. The path then runs through more open country between hedges to lead you through a gate. Bear a little right along a gravel track to the main road. Turn left along the footway past Ampfield House to return to the White Horse.

Hamble
The Victory Inn

DIRECTIONS TO START: APPROACH VIA THE M27 AND EXIT AT JUNCTION 8. FOLLOW THE SIGNS FOR HAMBLE. **PARKING:** DRIVE INTO THE VILLAGE TO THE FREE CAR PARK IN THE SQUARE ON YOUR LEFT.

Hamble is famous throughout the world as a yachting centre, but the village has another claim to fame. From earliest times the villagers have preserved their beautiful and historic Common, claiming their rights to graze cattle and cut gorse for fuel. As a result it has remained unimproved grassland, exceptionally rich in wildlife. The route of this walk explores the Common, following well-signed paths beside the river estuary to Southampton Water. Woodland paths through contrasting scenery lead us back to the village.

The Victory Inn

Beside the picturesque High Street leading to the quay you will find the Victory, a splendid pub that really lives up to its name. For as you walk through the porch into the oak-beamed bar of this 300 year old pub you feel you are stepping onto the deck of a man o'war. Reminders of the great fighting ships of Nelson's navy surround you including a magnificent mural depicting the battle of Trafalgar. A reminder of a more recent victory is a table top on which commandos about to embark on D-Day have carved their names.

Well-kept real ales are Ringwood. London Pride, Flowers Original and Directors and there is an excellent wine list. Fresh fish is the speciality of the house and when we called fish dishes included moules marinière and whole red mullet. The menu also lists steaks and home-made pies and Fajitas – strips of chicken breast or fillet beef coated in the pub's secret Fajita spices with peppers and onions.

The pub is open every day from 11 am to 11.30 pm (Sundays 10.30 pm.) Food is served Mondays to Thursdays from 12 noon to 2.30 pm and from 7 pm to 9.30 pm. On Saturdays food is available from 12 noon to 9.30 pm and on Sundays from 12 noon to 8.30 pm Children and dogs are welcome and there is a patio garden. Telephone: 02380 453105.

The Walk

① Turn left from the car park to the narrowest part of the High Street which runs steeply downhill to the waterfront. On your right you pass the 17th century Old House, half-timbered and infilled with

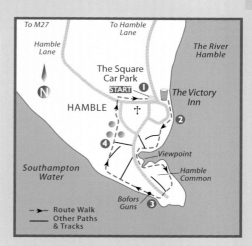

herringbone brickwork. Pass the Victory Inn on your left. The narrow street curves right at the foot to the public hard and quay. Bear right along the waterfront. Beside a grassy area you will see an anchor and plaque and beyond it a board giving 'Wartime Memories'. This commemorates US Naval Forces who built a dock in Hamble for landing craft as part of the preparations for D-Day. A little further on you come to a snack bar.

② Turn right and walk up a narrow twisting street, Ferry Hill, to Hamble Green. Turn left, following the footpath sign 'footpath to Hamble Common and the Coast'. This leads into woodland and information boards give details of the wildlife and history you will enjoy on this walk. Follow the circular walk signs and when the path divides take the left-hand path through woods to emerge on the open Common. Then the path bears left and shortly right to follow the shore round creeks coloured purple in summer with sea asters. Keep to the main path as it curves right under trees once more to a three-way signpost. Turn left, signed 'Hamble Point

The Hamble river.

via estuary'. The path continues beside the estuary then leads up steps. After about 50 yards go through a gate on the left and follow the path with woods and a fence on the left. Pass a stile on the left, then look for another gate on the left and make a detour through this gate to a magnificent viewpoint. Return to the circular route and follow the path through the trees to open common land joining a track from the right. Go through a gate, ignore a footpath sign to Hamble and cross the road to the

foreshore at Hamble Point. Now you enjoy fine views of Southampton Water.

③ Turn right along the shingle to the Second World War Bofors gun. Leave the gun on your left and follow the narrow path along the waterside. When you come to a wide grassy area turn right as directed across the grass, then through woods. Take the left-hand path at a division to a three-way finger post.

④ Keep straight ahead, signed 'Hamble Copse'. Continue through the copse to a minor road. Turn left to walk up to the main road, Hamble Lane. Turn right, past the church, to return to your car.

PLACES OF INTEREST NEARBY
Manor Farm Country Park is a beautiful area for walks and picnics. Telephone: 01489 787055.

Durley
The Farmer's Home

MAP: OS PATHFINDER 1284 (GR 516161)   **WALK 17**   **DISTANCE:** 3 MILES

DIRECTIONS TO START: DURLEY IS 2 MILES EAST OF THE B3354 BETWEEN BOTLEY AND FAIR OAK. TAKE THE TURNING FOR DURLEY, AND TURN RIGHT FOLLOWING THE SIGN FOR THE FARMER'S HOME. **PARKING:** PATRONS MAY LEAVE THEIR CARS IN THE PUB CAR PARK WHILE THEY WALK – PLEASE ASK FIRST.

D urley lies among lush meadows and oak woods close to the upper reaches of the Hamble river. William Cobbett, the 19th century author of *Rural Rides*, who lived nearby at Botley, described Durley as 'one of the most obscure villages in this whole kingdom.' Today this attractive village may no longer be obscure but it remains very much as he would have known it, a peaceful haven within a network of narrow lanes. From Durley, this walk follows meadow paths through undulating downland to Durley Mill. A quiet lane leads us to the highlight of the walk, a beautiful woodland path along a hillside above the Hamble valley. More meadow paths take us back to our starting point, the Farmer's Home pub.

The Farmer's Home

This typical friendly family country pub was originally, as its name suggests, a farmhouse. A small porch leads into comfortable bar areas with oak-beamed ceilings and large open fireplaces with blazing log fires in cold weather. The separate restaurant is equally welcoming. Real ales are Ringwood, London Pride and HSB. From the wide à la carte choice you could opt for chicken in brandy and mushroom sauce or king prawn thermidor. The Bar and Garden Menu ranges from omelettes and ploughman's platters to chargrilled pork steaks and Scotch beef curry. The pub offers a special welcome to children who have their own menu.

Opening times are 11 am to 3 pm and 6 pm to 11 pm during the week and all day on Saturdays and Sundays. Food is served from 12 noon to 2 pm and from 6.30 pm to 9 pm. (Sundays until 8 pm.) There is a large garden with swings, slides and a trampoline for children. Telephone: 01489 860457.

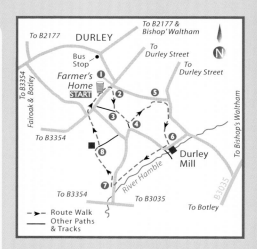

The Walk

① Turn left from the front of the pub and walk along Heathen Street for about 150 yards. Just before you come to a crossroads, turn right over a stile.

② Beyond the stile, walk past a house and garden on the right and cross another stile. Follow the meadow path ahead with a fence on your left. Over the next stile you cross a small bridge and a stile. Keep ahead beside the meadow with a hedge on your right. Cross another small bridge to meet a crosspath.

③ Turn left, hedge on the left, and follow the path as it rises to a stony track.

④ Bear left over a stile and keep ahead, hedge on the right, to cross double stiles and continue to a wooded area. Follow the right-hand fence and cross a stile into a meadow. Bear a little left to pass a house on your left and cross the stile to a lane.

⑤ Turn right and follow the lane to a T-junction where you turn right again, signed Curdridge. After about ¼ mile when the lane turns sharply left, take the narrow path on the right along the top of a wooded hillside. When you come to a fence climb some steps on the left, cross a stile and keep ahead beside a field, hedge on the right, to go over a stile to a track. Bear left for a few yards to a lane.

⑥ Turn right past Durley Mill which stands on the site of one of three mills mentioned in the Domesday Book. The present mill dates from the 1600s and continued working until 1965. Ignore the first footpath sign on the left (leading to a

A path through the woods in the Upper Hamble valley.

bridge) but turn left at the next footpath sign. Over a stile, the woodland path leads slightly right to run along the top of a hillside sloping down to the marshes of the Upper Hamble river. You leave the trees to go over a stile into a meadow. Follow the

PLACES OF INTEREST NEARBY

Hampshire Farm Museum, Manor Farm, Botley. A splendid reconstruction of life on a farm at the end of the 19th century. Open 10 am to 6 pm (5 pm in winter) from April to December. Weekends only in January and February. Telephone: 01489 787055.

green arrow footpath signs to continue beside meadows and over stiles to a lane.

⑦ Turn right for about 100 yards then take the gravel track on the left for Hill Farm. The track curves right to leave the farm on the left. After passing a private road and buildings on the left, the track divides.

⑧ Take the left-hand path which descends to a stile. Cross and keep ahead, keeping a hedge on your left. Over a stream, the path crosses the meadow to take you over a stile to a lane. Turn right to walk back to the Farmer's Home.

Bishop's Waltham
The Bunch of Grapes

MAP: OS PATHFINDER 1284 (GR 554175)	**WALK 18**	DISTANCE: 3 MILES

DIRECTIONS TO START: BISHOP'S WALTHAM LIES AT THE INTERSECTION OF THE B2177 AND THE B3035 EAST OF SOUTHAMPTON. **PARKING:** IN THE CLEARLY SIGNED BASINGWELL CAR PARK.

Bishop's Waltham is an enchanting small town, its narrow streets lined with gabled medieval houses and neat 18th century dwellings. It has all the quiet charm and friendly atmosphere of a village and many residents consider it to be so. Our walk starts from the car park near the church then follows meadow paths to a beautiful downland valley crossed by woodland tracks. Paths through an interesting nature reserve lead back to the town.

The Bunch of Grapes

There are so many delightful pubs and inns in Bishop's Waltham that it seems unfair to recommend just one. You will have no difficulty in finding a hostelry to suit! One place I have particularly enjoyed visiting is a tiny pub in St Peter's Street, close to the church, called the Bunch of Grapes. Old and beamed, it is a real country pub, unspoilt by time and still serving beers from the stillage behind the bar. No food is available but this is an excellent port of call if you have a picnic with you. Enjoy a drink with your food either in the cosy bar or in the pleasant garden. The Bunch of Grapes was one of the first pubs to be included in the CAMRA *Good Beer Guide* and offers Courage Best, Ushers Best and seasonal ales. Open 12 noon to 2 pm and 6 pm to 11 pm all week, Sundays 12 noon to 2 pm and 7 pm to 10.30 pm. Telephone: 01489 892935.

For outstanding coffee, tea and light lunches visit The Anvil nearby, a beautifully restored medieval house. The lunch menu offers delicious home-made soup and a variety of filled baguettes and sandwiches including smoked salmon and honey roast ham. Real Cornish cream teas are a speciality. Open every day except Monday, 10 am to 5 pm. Telephone: 01489 892969.

The Walk

① Walk through the car park to the far left hand corner past the Bishops Waltham Social Club on your left. Pass The Anvil on the corner of Houchin Street and cross Bank Street to walk up picturesque St Peter's Street past The Bunch of Grapes. Go through the churchyard gates and walk up to the south porch of St Peter's church. The

church is particularly spacious with an early 18th century gallery and a fine wooden pulpit dated 1626. Leave the church porch on your left along a gravel track which brings you out of the churchyard by the rectory on your left. Turn right to the main road.

② Turn left along the road for about 100 yards, turn right down Colville Drive and keep to Colville Drive as it curves left past Rareridge Lane. Bear right down a narrow hedged path to go through a gate into a meadow. Keep ahead across the middle of the meadow over the next stile aiming for a belt of trees.

③ Go through a gate on the left and walk through the trees to emerge on an open hillside. Turn right and follow the path along the hillside, taking the upper path at a division to enter woods where the path divides again at a gate. Follow the left-hand path which runs through the trees to a crosspath. (On the left the path descends to a stile.) Turn right and climb steps to a field. Keep ahead and at the other side of the field bear a little right to follow a hedged track which curves left to a lane.

Some of the splendid countryside around Bishop's Waltham.

④ Follow the lane for about 200 yards then turn left and almost immediately right along a green lane to the main road. Bear right along the pavement for about 150 yards then take the lane on the left signed 'right of way' by the Bishops Waltham village sign.

⑤ When the track swings left, keep straight on then keep to the track as it curves right to a gate. Just before the gate take the footpath on the right and go through a gate. A pleasant path leads through the trees. Go through a gate into a meadow. Keep ahead, go through another gate and continue with

a fenced playing field on your right. Go through the next gate and shortly after go through a small wooden gate on your left and turn right to walk through part of the Moors Nature Reserve. Just before a netted boardwalk go through a wooden gate on your right and resume your former heading to a road. Cross, and follow the footpath ahead to a main road.

⑥ Turn left and continue past the police station.

⑦ Turn right up Free Street and after about 50 yards bear left, following the sign for the library. Leave the library on your right and follow the footpath as it curves right to St Peter's churchyard. Follow the path beside a wall on the left, turn left through the churchyard gates and retrace your steps to the car park.

PLACES OF INTEREST NEARBY

Bishop's Waltham Palace: impressive ruins of a great medieval house. Open daily 10 am to 6 pm (5 pm in winter). Telephone: 01962 777406.

Itchen Abbas
The Trout Inn

MAP: OS PATHFINDER 1243 (GR 536329)   **WALK 19**   **DISTANCE:** 3 MILES

DIRECTIONS TO START: ITCHEN ABBAS IS BESIDE THE B3047 BETWEEN WINCHESTER AND ALRESFORD. THE TROUT INN STANDS PROMINENTLY BESIDE THE MAIN ROAD. **PARKING:** PATRONS MAY LEAVE THEIR CARS IN THE PUB CAR PARK WHILE WALKING PROVIDED PERMISSION IS REQUESTED.

From its source near Hinton Ampner, the river Itchen flows west towards Winchester, creating one of the loveliest of Hampshire's many river valleys. The clear water divides into several streams as it meanders through fertile watermeadows which have attracted settlers from earliest times. So as you walk through the valley today you discover villages with clusters of thatched, half-timbered houses and churches where people have worshipped for over 900 years. This walk follows the river to explore three delightful villages and enjoy the wildlife which flourishes in these peaceful surroundings. Besides the fish for which the river is famous it is home for a wealth of waterbirds including swans, wild ducks, coots and moorhens.

The Trout Inn

We start a stone's throw from the river in Itchen Abbas. A former coaching inn on the route between London and Winchester, the Trout has preserved the atmosphere of a traditional family inn catering for everyone. You will find a spacious and comfortable bar area where you can enjoy a meal or snack, a non-smoking dining room and a special room for walkers, complete with maps. As you would expect, the inn has a fishing theme, with rods, nets and haversacks much in evidence. The walls also feature paintings by local artists for sale at very reasonable prices. The Trout is well known for its traditional Hampshire recipes such as gammon in sherry sauce and pheasant pie in a rich red wine sauce. Real ales are Speckled Hen, IPA and there is always a guest beer. The cider is Strongbow and there is an extensive wine list. Opening times Mondays to Saturdays are from 12 noon to 3 pm and from 6 pm to 11 pm. Sundays the pub is open from 12 noon to 11 pm. Food is served Mondays to Saturdays from 12 noon to 2.15 pm and from 6.30 pm to 9 pm. On Sundays food is available from 12 noon to 8 pm.

Dogs on leads and children are welcome. But – the landlord insists – he will admit only well-behaved grannies! Outside there is a pleasant garden and a children's play area. Overnight accommodation is offered and day fishing and golf can be arranged nearby. Telephone: 01962 779537.

The Walk

① Leave the front of the Trout Inn on your right, cross the road and turn down

the lane ahead, signed 'To the Church'. The church, on your right, was rebuilt in Victorian times but original 11th century stonework can be seen in the porch and chancel arch.

② Just before the churchyard gate, turn right to leave the church on your left. Walk up a grassy path then follow the narrow path through a small wooden gate to continue over a meadow which slopes down to the river on your left. Go through a gate to cross a drive then through another gate opening to meadows. If you look downhill you will see a small copse close to the river. A plaque states that this was the site of a cottage owned by Viscount Grey of Falloden, Liberal Foreign Secretary from 1905 to 1916. He found the cottage 'a lovely refuge'. Beside the plaque we found a wreath of flowers in memory of his friend, the naturalist and author W.H.Hudson, who recorded happy hours spent in the cottage in his book *Hampshire Days*.

③ Go through a gate and follow the path as it runs closer to the river, continues beside the hedged gardens of Chilland

The River Itchen.

House and becomes gravelled. Descend steps to a lane.

④ Turn left for a few yards then turn right, following the footpath sign. A clearly signed path leads through gates and over meadows to a lane opposite Martyr Worthy church. Turn left down the lane then continue along the footpath ahead to cross the long footbridge over the river. This is a place to linger. The river flows wide and free between banks of flowers and rushes, shadowed by willows and alders full of

PLACES OF INTEREST NEARBY
The historic **Mid-Hants Steam Railway** runs over 10 miles between Alresford and Alton, with intermediate stations at Medstead and Ropley. Telephone: 01962 733810.

birdsong. Keep to the narrow footpath which winds on over a smaller bridge and through a gate.

⑤ Cross the meadow ahead, aiming for a large thatched house. Just before the house turn right to leave the house on your left then go through a gate on your left and follow a gravel track to a lane.

⑥ Turn left and follow the grass-bordered lane for about ⅓ mile to a footpath sign on the left. Follow the sign left along a track which recrosses the Itchen to a gravel track which passes Chilland Mill (notice the old iron hitching ring on the wall) to the foot of Chilland Lane. Walk up the lane to meet the steps on the right leading to our earlier path at point 4. Turn right to retrace your route to Itchen Abbas and the Trout Inn.

Hinton Ampner
The Hinton Arms

DIRECTIONS TO START: HINTON AMPNER IS ABOUT 9 MILES EAST OF WINCHESTER BESIDE THE A272. **PARKING:** PATRONS MAY LEAVE THEIR CARS IN THE PUB CAR PARK WHILE WALKING – PLEASE ASK FIRST.

Beautiful views over the South Downs are an outstanding feature of this walk. The route starts in the tiny hamlet of Hinton Ampner and crosses the parkland surrounding a fine Neo-Georgian house before following the crest of a downland ridge. North of the ridge, the land rises to Lamborough Fields, the site of the Civil War battle of Cheriton. Field paths lead us north to cross the valley and take Cheriton Lane, a wide grassy track running along the hillside close to the site of the battle. Our route touches the outskirts of Cheriton village before turning south to return to Hinton Ampner.

The Hinton Arms

This friendly former coaching inn has welcomed travellers for over 150 years. The heavily beamed ceiling is decorated with hundreds of beer mugs and farm tools. You can enjoy a snack at the bar or a full meal in one of the two eating areas, one of which is non-smoking. Light bites include hoagie rolls, soft wholemeal baguettes, with fillings such as beef and apple or prawn and mayonnaise. Examples of dishes that might be found on the specials board are pork chops with cream and mushrooms and poached salmon with lemon and herb butter, with treacle and walnut tart among the sweets.

Several reals ales are available including Ringwood Best and four specially brewed for the Hinton Arms by Hampshire Brewery in Romsey. Opening times are 9.30 am to 3 pm and from 5 pm to 12 pm. The pub is open all day on Saturdays and Sundays. Food is served from 11 am to 2.30 pm and from 6 pm to 10 pm. There is a pleasant patio and garden and a meadow with swings for children. Telephone: 01962 771252.

The Walk

① Turn right from the pub entrance along the grassy verge beside the A272. Cross the drive to Hinton Ampner House and about 60 yards further turn right by the footpath sign and cross a stile.

② There is no clear path at this point but with your back to the stile bear half-left over the grass towards the drive leading to Hinton Ampner House. About 50 yards before you come to the drive bear left towards an ornamental urn on a pedestal.

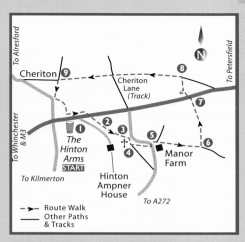

With the urn around 30 yards or so on your right keep ahead to go over a stile by a gate to a narrow lane.

③ Turn right to go past some entrance gates. The church of All Saints is on your right. Dating from Saxon times, it retains some typical long and short stonework. From the church there is a splendid view of Hinton Ampner House.

④ A few yards past the entrance gates turn left to leave Church Cottages on your left and go through a gate. Ignore the footpath sign pointing right and keep straight on (unsigned) and walk beside a meadow with a fence on your left. The path leads along the top of a hill with fine views. Go through a gate to a lane opposite Manor Farm. Turn left for a few yards then turn right, following a bridleway sign. When the track curves left keep straight ahead past a gate.

⑤ Follow the meadow path ahead with a hedge on your left for a little over $^1/_4$ mile to the next hedge.

Hinton Ampner House.

⑥ Turn immediately left to walk downhill with a hedge on your right to the A272.

⑦ Turn left for a few yards and cross the road to a stile on the other side. Go over the stile and keep ahead with a fence on your left to a crosspath. Turn left and continue for about 40 yards. Now turn right before an iron gate and immediately right again. Turn left, with the hedge on your left, and walk up the side of a field to go through a gate and meet a hedged crosstrack, Cheriton Lane.

⑧ Turn left under a height barrier to follow this wide way for a mile, keeping straight ahead over all crosstracks. Continue under a height barrier and about 50 yards further on you come to a narrow, tunnel-like path burrowing its way downhill on the left. Some garden fencing is on the corner.

⑨ Turn left down this path which broadens to meet a road. A few yards to your left you will see a small gate. Turn left and follow a narrow path to cross a stile into a meadow. The Hinton Arms is directly ahead. Walk down the meadow, hedge on your right, to return to the pub.

PLACES OF INTEREST NEARBY

Hinton Ampner House (NT) contains a wonderful collection of furniture and paintings and the gardens are some of the finest in Hampshire. Open 1.30 pm to 5.30 pm from Easter to September, gardens daily except Monday, Thursday and Friday (open Bank Holiday Mondays), house on Tuesdays and Wednesdays plus weekends in August. Telephone: 01962 771305.

Little London
The Plough Inn

MAP: OS PATHFINDERS 1204, 1188 (GR 622598)	WALK 21	DISTANCE: 3 MILES

DIRECTIONS TO START: LITTLE LONDON IS A SMALL VILLAGE ABOUT 7 MILES NORTH OF BASINGSTOKE. THE BEST APPROACH IS VIA THE A340 ALDERMASTON-BASINGSTOKE ROAD. AT PAMBER END TURN OFF THE A340 FOLLOWING THE SIGN FOR BRAMLEY. AFTER ABOUT A MILE TURN LEFT FOLLOWING THE SIGN FOR SILCHESTER ROMAN TOWN. CONTINUE FOR ABOUT ¾ MILE THROUGH LITTLE LONDON TO THE PLOUGH INN WHICH IS ON YOUR LEFT. **PARKING:** PATRONS MAY LEAVE THEIR CARS IN THE PUB CAR PARK WHILE THEY WALK – PLEASE ASK FIRST.

The ancient woodlands of Pamber Forest were once part of the great Royal Forest of Windsor. The route of this walk follows paths through the heart of these beautiful woods. The branches of ancient oak trees arch overhead, wild daffodils bloom in the hazel coppices in spring and wetter areas are rich in orchids. In summer, butterflies include the silver washed fritillary and the white admiral. Roe deer can be seen, especially at dusk feeding beside the grassy tracks. This wealth of wildlife is partly due to the reintroduction in some areas of coppicing, an old form of woodland management which creates more open areas. We pass some of these on our walk.

The Plough Inn

The Plough is a small, very friendly village inn with a warm welcome for everyone. It is over 350 years old with timbered ceilings and blazing log fires in chilly weather. At one time the owner also ran a nearby brickworks and they have been put to good use at the Plough for floors and partitions. Don't miss the framed will of Joseph Holloway, dealer in 'bricks and tiles'. He was born in 1773 and died in 1857 and as well as his will there is a fascinating account of his life. Tucked away in this remote corner of Hampshire close to Pamber Forest the Plough is the perfect place to relax after your walk. The inn offers a varied range of real ales including Ringwood Best. Delicious rolls and baguettes are available with crusty bread and generous fillings including chicken, bacon and sweetcorn and roast pork and stuffing. Opening times are from 12 noon to 2.30 pm (3 pm at weekends) and from 5.30 pm to 11 pm. Food is available from 12 noon to 2 pm and from 5.30 pm to 9 pm. (6 pm to 11 pm at weekends).

There is a pleasant, enclosed garden just right for a drink on a summer evening. Telephone: 01256 850628.

The Walk

① Turn left from the front door of the pub and take the footpath almost immediately on your left. The path runs between high hedges with a wood on your right through a gate to an open meadow. Keep ahead then follow the path as it bears very slightly left over the meadow to a crosspath.

② Turn right and follow the path which leads over the meadow to a stile by a gate.

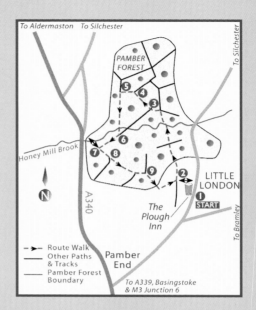

Cross the stile to follow a beautiful grassy path into Pamber Forest. Keep to this path ignoring all side paths for about ³/₄ mile to a post on your left marked with coloured bands indicating a waymarked walk. (We touch on this only occasionally as our walk is a little longer.)

③ Turn left along the waymarked path and keep straight on over a crosspath. After about ¹/₄ mile you come to a T-junction.

④ Bear left to more crosspaths in front of a wooden barrier.

⑤ Turn left to leave the barrier on your right and follow the path through the trees with the edge of the forest at first on your right. The path narrows, crosses a small wooden bridge over the tiny Honey Mill brook and continues to a wide crosspath.

⑥ Bear right to the barrier at the western entrance to the forest. Do not go past the

In Pamber Forest.

barrier but retrace your steps for about 30 yards to a division. Your earlier path is on the left.

⑦ This time take the right hand path and keep ahead for about 150 yards.

⑧ The path divides again. Follow the left hand path which becomes a wide embanked way leading through the forest glades towards the south-west corner of the woods. As you approach the forest boundary keep to the main path which curves left past a smaller path on the right to a division.

⑨ Turn right and follow the path to leave the forest through a gate to the meadow we crossed early in our walk. Follow the path ahead over the grass which soon bears slightly left to bring you to the crosspath at 2. Retrace your steps over the meadow to return to the Plough Inn and your car.

Silchester
The Calleva Arms

MAP: OS PATHFINDER 1188 (GR 628621) | **WALK 22** | **DISTANCE:** 3 MILES

DIRECTIONS TO START: SILCHESTER IS ABOUT 9 MILES NORTH OF BASINGSTOKE. THE BEST APPROACH IS VIA THE A340 ALDERMASTON-BASINGSTOKE ROAD. AT PAMBER END TURN RIGHT FOR BRAMLEY AND THEN LEFT THROUGH LITTLE LONDON TO SILCHESTER. THE CALLEVA ARMS IS ON YOUR LEFT. **PARKING:** PATRONS MAY LEAVE THEIR CARS IN THE PUB CAR PARK WHILE THEY WALK – PLEASE ASK FIRST. ALTERNATIVELY, PARK ON THE ROAD.

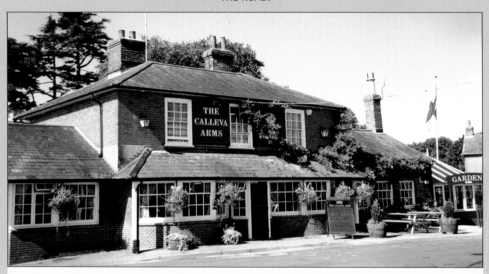

A thousand years of history come alive as you follow this walk from present-day Silchester, its houses scattered around a wide common in Saxon fashion, to the gleaming white walls of a great Roman town. The Romans built their town over part of the site of a large Iron Age settlement inhabited by a Celtic tribe, the Atrebates. From being a small military outpost established about AD 45 the town developed into an important administrative centre governing an area of around the size of Berkshire. Excavations have revealed the remains of a forum surrounded by public buildings and shops, a basilica, three temples, impressive houses and a tiny Christian church dating from the 4th century AD. Today most of these remains are grassed over but the splendid city walls, dating from the 3rd century, are still a thrilling sight, rising in places to over 20 feet. Our walk crosses the central area of the town before following the walls to return to our starting point, the Calleva Arms.

The Calleva Arms

The pub is named after the Roman name for the town, Calleva Atrebatum, the capital of the Atrebates. Attractively situated overlooking Silchester common, the Calleva Arms is a bright, modern building with a large bar area and separate games room. But it is still a genuine village pub decorated with carved wood figures and farm implements. Nor are the Romans forgotten. There are panels on the walls depicting Roman soldiers and pictures of some of the finds discovered during excavations of the town including a fine mosaic pavement.

Opening hours on Monday to Friday are from 11 am to 3 pm and 5.30 pm to 11 pm, on Saturday from 11 am to 11 pm and on Sunday from 12 noon to 10.30 pm. Meals are served from 12 noon to 2 pm and from 6.30 pm to 9 pm. Tempting dishes include homemade pies, natural crumb plaice fillet, luxury chicken Kiev and a wide choice of salads. Ingredients are locally sourced where possible. Real ales are Gale's HSB, and Butser, GB and a guest ale. Strongbow and Scrumpy Jack cider are available on draught and the wine list includes all Gale's fruit wines. There is a beautiful garden and a petanque court. Dogs on leads are allowed in the bar area outside mealtimes. Telephone: 01189 700305.

The Walk

① With your back to the pub entrance cross the grass ahead, turn right over the road and walk down Whistler's Lane to a T-junction.

② Turn left and follow the lane to a bridleway sign on the right beside the Calleva Museum. Bear right along a track, leaving the museum on your left. Cross a stile to continue along a footpath between paddocks. The path becomes hedged and curves right. Go through a small gate to face the low eastern wall of the Roman town.

③ Turn left along a wide track which shortly bears right and leads for about 1/2 mile over the central area of the town towards the barns of Manor Farm and the pointed bell turret of St Mary the Virgin church.

④ Follow the sign to turn right round a barn then left to enter the churchyard. The little church is built on the site of a Roman temple just within the north-eastern corner of the walls. There is much to enjoy inside including a beautiful 16th century chancel screen graced with a frieze of angels. Turn right from the church porch, go through a small gate and turn right past a pond on the left. Now you will see the full height of the walls.

Part of the impressive Roman wall at Silchester.

⑤ Keep the walls close on your right and continue beside them over a track past a wooden gate. Walk beside the walls as they curve right. Information boards give details of their construction and indicate gateways. Just past the southern gateway a board indicates the remains of the Iron Age

settlement. Keep beside the walls as the path narrows to lead through a gate and meet our earlier path at point 3. Turn left and retrace your steps until you come to the museum on your right.

⑥ Ignore the gravel track opposite but turn left for a few yards and take the narrow footpath on the right. This takes you through the trees to the road by the war memorial. Turn left to the Calleva Arms.

PLACES OF INTEREST NEARBY

Silchester (Calleva) Museum presents an excellent picture of the growth of the Roman town. Guidebook and leaflet available. For opening times telephone: 01734 700362. Most of the discoveries made during excavations are housed in Reading Museum.

Eversley
The Golden Pot

MAP OS PATHFINDER 1188 (SOME ROAD NUMBERS HAVE BEEN CHANGED) (GR 788617)

WALK 23

DISTANCE: 2½ MILES

DIRECTIONS TO START: EVERSLEY STRETCHES FOR ALMOST 2 MILES BESIDE THE A327, AS IT RUNS BETWEEN READING TO MEET THE A30 NEAR HARTLEY WITNEY, AND THE B3272 BETWEEN THE A327 AND YATELEY. TURN EASTWARDS OFF THE A327 PASS CHURCH LANE ON YOUR LEFT AND TURN RIGHT ALONG THE B3272 TO EVERSLEY CENTRE. THE GOLDEN POT IS ON YOUR LEFT. **PARKING:** PATRONS MAY USE THE PUB CAR PARK WHILE THEY WALK – PLEASE ASK FIRST.

Charles Kingsley's novel *The Water Babies*, must be one of the most loved and widely read books in our language. This walk in the valley of the river Blackwater starts from Eversley where Kingsley was Rector from 1844 to 1875 and continues past the Rectory where he began the novel in 1863 and the church of Blessed Mary the Virgin where he preached. Today he is remembered in Eversley with deep affection for the care he gave his parishioners. This included founding a school which still bears his name. The tranquil meadows and oak woods around Eversley can have changed little since Kingsley's time and I am sure you will enjoy this walk in the great writer's footsteps.

The Golden Pot

Our starting point is a charming pub, the Golden Pot. Originally it was two cottages, one of which dates from the early 17th century. Inside, you are made to feel a welcome guest in a cosy and very comfortable home. Although deservedly popular there is room for everyone with plenty of quiet corners where you can relax and enjoy your meal or drink. The menu includes Thai fishcakes with sweet chilli dressing and noodles, and baked salmon in parchment. A Golden Pot speciality is Swiss Rosti, a delicious blend of bacon, onions, eggs and cheese served in a variety of ways. Monday evening is a special 'Rosti night'. Real ales are Greene King and other keg beers. Opening times from Monday to Saturday are 11 am to 3 pm and from 5.30 pm to 11 pm. Sundays from 12 noon to 3 pm. The pub is closed Sunday evenings. Meals are served from 12 noon to 2.15 pm (Sundays 2 pm) and in the bar only on Mondays and Saturdays. In the evenings meals are served in the bar from 6 pm to 9.15 pm and in the restaurant from 7 pm to 9.15 pm. Families are welcome and there is a pleasant garden overlooking meadows and woods. Telephone: 01189 700305.

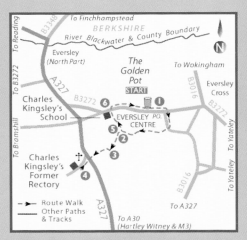

The Walk

① Turn left from the front of the pub, cross the road and walk through the village, passing the post office on your right. Turn right down Hollybush Lane and when the lane curves left ignore the footpath leading ahead towards Hollybush Farm and take the footpath on the right to go through a swing gate and follow a meadow path. As you approach woodland you meet a wider crosstrack. Bear a little right to continue along a narrow path past an iron gate with the woods on your left. At the end of the wood continue along the path between hedges to cross a plank bridge and a stile.

② Keep ahead for about 40 yards then follow the hedge round to the left to walk beside a field and cross a stile.

③ Turn right beside a line of splendid oak trees – look for little owls here – and continue over another stile to go through a small wooden gate to a road. Cross the road, and walk over the grass ahead to the entrance to the churchyard on your right. This is Kingsley's church approached by an avenue of yews which he planted. His grave is close to the path on the left. Inside, a beautiful window in the chancel commemorates the centenary of his arrival. It shows St Elizabeth of Hungary, the subject of one of his poems, with a Water Baby either side of her. From the entrance to the churchyard walk a little further down the

The Rectory, once the home of Charles Kingsley.

lane to see his rectory, part of which is Elizabethan, on your right.

④ Retrace your steps past the church on your left over the grass and the meadows to meet our earlier path by the stile at point 2.

⑤ Do not cross the stile but bear half-left over the meadow to go through an iron swing gate. Take the narrow path ahead to cross an estate road and continue to a minor road.

⑥ Turn left to the entrance to Charles Kingsley's School. On the iron gates you

will see a little figure of the chimney sweep, Tom from *The Water Babies*. Turn right to walk back to the Golden Pot.

PLACES OF INTEREST NEARBY

Wellington Country Park, to the west, is ideal for family visits. Open March to October daily and at weekends in winter, 10 am to 5.30 pm. Telephone: 01734 326444.

Stratfield Saye, west of the A33, is a Jacobean house, the former home of the Duke of Wellington. Open from May to the last Sunday in September, daily except Friday. Tel: 01256 882882.

Odiham
The Waterwitch

DIRECTIONS TO START: ODIHAM IS ABOUT 6 MILES EAST OF BASINGSTOKE BESIDE THE A287. DRIVE INTO THE TOWN AND TURN DOWN COLT HILL, SIGNED FOR THE WATERWITCH AND THE BASINGSTOKE CANAL. THE PUB IS ON YOUR LEFT JUST BEFORE COLT BRIDGE. **PARKING:** PATRONS MAY LEAVE THEIR CARS IN THE PUB CAR PARK WHILE WALKING – PLEASE ASK PERMISSION. THERE IS ALSO A PUBLIC CAR PARK JUST OVER COLT BRIDGE.

A stroll beside the Basingstoke Canal and paths through old oak woods combine to make this a superb walk. The canal was completed in 1794 to transport timber and farm produce from Basingstoke via the Wey Navigation and the river Thames to London. After becoming derelict, restoration work began in 1973 and now it provides a beautiful tree-shaded waterway with over 30 miles of towpath for walkers. We leave the canal to walk through the woods of Dogmersfield Park and then take meadow paths to return to the canal and the Waterwitch pub, our starting point.

The Waterwitch

Named after a barge that used to carry coal between London and Basingstoke, this pub is very much a part of the history of the canal. It dates from the 16th century and there is an old well in the bar. Families are specially welcome and have their own dining area. The menu offers something for everyone: breast of chicken in a creamy bacon and mushroom sauce, for example, as well as home-made lasagnes and curries and doorstep sandwiches – a meal in themselves! Real ales include Theakstons, H.S.B. and T.E.A. Strongbow and Woodpecker ciders are available and there is an extensive wine list.

Opening times during the week are from 12 noon to 11 pm. Meals are served from 12 noon to 10 pm, (Sundays 9.30 pm). There is a delightful canalside garden. Telephone: 01256 702778.

The Walk

① From the pub entrance turn left to cross Colt Bridge. Turn right to walk down to the towpath. Follow the towpath – canal on your right – to go under the A287. Continue beside the canal which runs through attractive open countryside. Walk round a gate and keep ahead to go under Broad Oak Bridge.

② Turn immediately left to climb the bank, walk round a wooden gate and turn left to cross the bridge.

③ After about 30 yards turn left, following a sign, over the grass. The path may be faint at first but soon becomes clearer as it enters woodland. Continue through the trees with the canal a few yards away on your left.

④ Bear right to follow a beautiful path through the oak woods of Dogmersfield Forest Park. Pass a footpath on the right and when the woods cease keep ahead along a grassy path to a footpath sign in front of lodge gates. Turn right and follow the path for a few yards to the A287.

⑤ Cross the road, turn left for about 40 yards and take the footpath just to the left of a drive and continue through the woods for about 1/4 mile.

⑥ Look carefully on the right for a narrow plank bridge and stile and cross them to a gravel track. Bear left following the signs along a path which curves right round the foot of a paddock then continues to a stile. Cross the stile and keep ahead beside a meadow with a hedge on your left.

⑦ As you near the other end of the meadow you will see a stile on the left. Cross this and bear a little right, aiming for the corner of a hedge. Keep the same

The Basingstoke Canal.

heading to continue over the meadow and cross the next stile.

⑧ Bear right to cross a wooden causeway

PLACES OF INTEREST NEARBY

Odiham Castle (remains) can be reached by crossing Colt Bridge and walking to the left for about 2 miles.

Basingstoke Canal. To find out more visit the Basingstoke Visitor Canal Centre in Mytchett Place Road, Mytchett, Surrey. Telephone: 01252 370073. The narrow boat John Pinkerton offers trips on the canal from April to June.

over a stream and walk beside a meadow with a hedge on your right. After about ¼ mile, (before you come to a stile about 50 yards ahead) look for a black iron gate on the right.

⑨ Turn right through the gate to continue beside a line of trees through another iron gate and beside another field to emerge on a minor road. Cross over, climb the stile ahead and follow the footpath over a stile along a narrow footpath to the Colt Hill road. Turn right to return to the Waterwitch and your car.

Upton Grey
The Hoddington Arms

MAP: OS PATHFINDER 1224 (GR 699483)   **WALK 25**   **DISTANCE:** 2½ MILES

DIRECTIONS TO START: UPTON GREY IS ABOUT 10 MILES SOUTH-EAST OF BASINGSTOKE. APPROACHING FROM THE NORTH LEAVE THE M3 AT JUNCTION 5, TAKING THE A287. TURN RIGHT ALONG THE B3349 TO SOUTH WARNBOROUGH AND TURN RIGHT IN THE VILLAGE FOR UPTON GREY. APPROACHING FROM THE SOUTH VIA THE A31 TURN LEFT JUST PAST CHAWTON ALONG THE A339, THEN RIGHT AT SOUTHROPE, THROUGH WESTON PATRICK TO UPTON GREY **PARKING:** PATRONS MAY LEAVE THEIR CARS IN THE PUB CAR PARK WHILE THEY WALK – PLEASE ASK FIRST.

Upton Grey, where this walk starts, is an enchanting village tucked neatly in a fold of the North Hampshire Downs. Many of the houses are half-timbered and thatched or built of old rose-coloured brick. In the centre of the village ducks paddle happily round a pond. We enjoy a look at the village then take a track which climbs gently to cross open downland. Field paths lead back to the village giving beautiful views over the rooftops to Hoddington House, framed by parkland.

The Hoddington Arms

Our starting point is the Hoddington Arms, a traditional country inn with a warm and friendly welcome. Three 18th century cottages have been sympathetically converted to form this listed old-world pub which features a bar area and two restaurants, one non-smoking. The non-smoking restaurant is particularly attractive. Originally a stable, the wooden partitions have been retained to form secluded dining areas decorated with horse brasses and harness. The fine cask ales, Ruddles Best, Old Speckled Hen and IPA, with a guest ale are kept to perfection and there is Strongbow cider and an extensive wine list. The menu features traditional dishes such as venison, game with port, rabbit and mushroom pies, fresh fish and steaks. Lighter meals include delicious home-made soup and a range of salads.

Opening times are from 12 noon to 3 pm and from 6 pm to 11 pm. Sundays from 12 noon to 4 pm and from 7 pm to 10.30 pm. Meals are served from 12 noon to 2 pm (Sundays 2.30 pm) and from 6.30 pm to 9 pm. No meals are served on Sunday evenings. The large, attractive garden has a safe enclosed playground for children. Telephone: 01256 862371.

The Walk

① Turn left from the frontage of the pub and continue through the village to the road junction by the pond. Bear right, leaving the pond on your left and following the sign for Tunworth. After about ¼ mile, before you come to the church, look for a footpath sign and narrow footpath by a brick wall on your right.

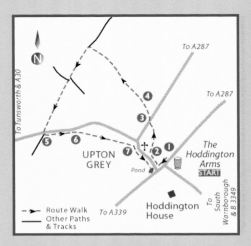

② Turn right along the path with the wall on your right. The path curves left and continues to meet a gravel track. Follow the track as it curves right then leave it and turn left through a gap in the hedge to a lane.

③ Cross the lane, bear right for a couple of yards, then cross a stile on the left. The path leads a little right over a meadow full of wild flowers in season, to another stile. Cross this and keep the same heading over the next meadow to pass a house on the left and go over a stile to a wide hedged track. This meets an asphalt path. Bear left for a few yards then follow the wide gravel track ahead indicated with a bridleway sign.

④ Follow this track as it climbs the down to a crosstrack. Turn left and follow this track for almost a mile with a high hedge on your left and downland fields on your right. Go straight over a crosstrack. When the broad white track you are following curves right keep straight on along a grassy path to meet the Tunworth road.

⑤ Turn left beside the road. In a little

Our path to the Downs.

under ¼ mile when the road begins to descend and curve left look for a footpath sign on the right.

⑥ Turn right as the sign directs with a hedge on your left. Walk down the side of

PLACES OF INTEREST NEARBY

Basing House at Old Basing, north of the A30. This great Tudor palace withstood a siege of two years by Cromwell's soldiers. Today the ruins still convey a good impression of the once magnificent mansion. Open April to September, Wednesday to Sunday, 2 pm to 6 pm. Telephone: 01256 467294.

the field, go through a small wood to continue downhill towards Upton Grey. The path meets a gravel track in front of houses. Turn left to rejoin the Tunworth road.

⑦ Bear right down the village. You pass the church on your left and it well repays a visit. The chancel is 12th century with deep-splayed single lancet windows. Outside, an oak tree has been planted in memory of Sir Winston Churchill who, a plaque states, had similar qualities! Turn left by the pond to return to the Hoddington Arms.

Kingsley
The Cricketers

MAP: OS PATHFINDER 1244 (GR 699483)   **WALK 26**   **DISTANCE:** 2½ MILES

DIRECTIONS TO START: KINGSLEY IS BESIDE THE B3004 ABOUT 6 MILES EAST OF ALTON. APPROACHING FROM THE A31 ALTON BYPASS FOLLOW SIGNS TO THE B3004 AND BORDON AND EVENTUALLY HEAD EAST THROUGH EAST WORLDHAM TO KINGSLEY. APPROACHING FROM THE EAST TURN FOR KINGSLEY FROM THE A325. THE CRICKETERS IS BESIDE THE B3004. **PARKING:** PATRONS MAY LEAVE THEIR CARS IN THE PUB CAR PARK WHILE THEY WALK.

Kingsley is now a large village with a scattering of attractive old cottages, but once it was a tiny huddle of huts in a clearing in the Royal Forest of Woolmer. This was a forest in the medieval sense, a large area of wild country with open heaths, marshes, scrub and woodland. Today you can still walk in this fascinating landscape following the route of this ramble on Kingsley Common, a small part of the once great forest that has survived the centuries. As well as the forest's historical interest, the ancient oak woods, sandy heaths and mires provide homes for a rich variety of wildlife.

The Cricketers

In an ideal situation beside the western edge of the Common, this is an inviting black and white building, originally a farmhouse. A document dated 1780 records that the occupants sold local produce to passers-by so establishing a tradition ably carried on today. For the Cricketers is a real country village pub where all, locals and visitors alike, receive the same friendly welcome. When the weather is cold you can draw up your chair beside a blazing log fire. There is a good range of real ales, cider is Strongbow and there is a varied wine list. Most of the food is home-cooked and favourites include steak and kidney pie and cottage pie served in the old-fashioned way out of deep dishes. Among the other choices when we called were tasty liver and bacon, chicken and mushroom tagliatelle in white wine sauce and gammon with egg or pineapple.

Opening times from Monday to Thursday are from 12 noon to 2.30 pm and from 4 pm to 11 pm. On Fridays and Saturdays the pub is open all day from 12 noon to 11 pm (Sundays 10.30 pm). Meals are served from 12 noon to 2 pm and from 6 pm to 9.30 pm. Dogs and children are welcome. There is a charming cottage garden, perfect for a warm summer afternoon, and a paddock for the children to run about in. If you plan to come as a group and eat after your walk, it is a good idea to order your meal before you set out. Telephone: 01420 476730.

The Walk

① Start this walk on the Common with a ramble around the beautiful pond just east of the Cricketers. Leave the front of the pub on your right, do not continue to the road, but turn right past the entrance to the car park to the large parking area beside the pond. Bear right through the trees to the water's edge then turn left on the narrow path along the bank with the pond on your right. A Site of Special Scientific Interest, the pond is delightful, bordered with reeds and bulrushes, shaded by oaks and willows and brilliant in summer with lilies. Follow the path round the pond until you reach a hard-surfaced track facing the Cricketer's car park.

② Turn left to pass Ockham Hall on the right and continue to a division.

③ Take the right-hand track, turn left at a footpath sign and right at the next sign to a stile by a gate. Cross and follow the meadow path ahead with a fence on your

Kingsley Common.

left and a golf course on your right. The path curves left beside the fence over a plank bridge to double stiles.

④ Cross the stiles and a concrete bridge over the Oxney stream and follow a narrow path which bears left over grassland. Pass a stile on your left and follow the good path ahead with a hedge now on your left to a stony track. Turn left to a concrete lane and turn left again over a wider bridge over the Oxney stream.

⑤ Follow the track to enter oak woods.

PLACES OF INTEREST NEARBY

Jane Austen's House, Chawton, off the A31 south of Alton. Here she revised her earlier novels and wrote the great works of her maturity. Opening times vary. Telephone: 01420 83262.

⑥ After about 40 yards turn right along the foot of a slope on your left and walk along the edge of the woods. Continue over an open sandy area to a joining track and bear right to walk past tracks on the left and right until you come to Riverside Cottage on your right. Turn left. The track curves right to an open area with houses on the right.

⑦ Take the first track on the left to walk through oak woods to a division. Continue along the left-hand track which leads past a barrier to a large grassy area. Keep ahead then bear slight right to follow a narrow path that burrows downhill through the gorse bushes then leads through scattered trees past the pond on your right to a T-junction. Turn right and follow the track to return to the Cricketers.

Hawkley
The Hawkley Inn

MAP: OS PATHFINDER 1265 (GR 748292)   **WALK 27**   **DISTANCE:** 3 MILES

DIRECTIONS TO START: HAWKLEY IS 5 MILES NORTH OF PETERSFIELD. THE BEST APPROACH IS VIA THE A3. TAKE THE TURNING FOR LISS THEN FOR WEST LISS. IN WEST LISS TURN LEFT FOLLOWING THE SIGN FOR HAWKLEY. AFTER ABOUT 2 MILES TURN LEFT FOLLOWING SIGNS FOR UPPER GREEN AND PRIORS DEAN. THE INN IS ON YOUR RIGHT.
PARKING: PARK IN THE LANE NEAR THE PUB.

Dramatic scenery and spectacular views are your reward on this superb walk in Hampshire's famous 'hanger' country-side. Hawkley lies in a quiet valley in the shade of one of the most beautiful of these steep, densely-wooded escarpments. It is a small, very attractive village, with houses neatly set around a green and an appealing Victorian church. Our walk leads through the woods along the foot of the hanger, then climbs gently to the top, a fine viewpoint. We descend the down into another valley beside a manor then take more woodland paths round the hanger to return to the village.

The Hawkley Inn

As you would expect in this remote countryside, the Hawkley Inn is a genuine, rustic village pub. The bar opens straight onto the village street, you are greeted with friendly nods and smiles and you enjoy your drink or meal at simple wooden tables. A moose with pink spectacles keeps an eye on the proceedings. But do not be deceived! This is a good food pub and a good ale pub. The sign outside displays the head of a moose so it is a 'free hoose'! Several of the excellent real ales are brewed locally and when we called the list included the intriguingly named Moose Drool as well as Ringwood Best and Ballards Best. Home-made cider is available in summer and there is a choice of seven wines. Among more usual dishes such as spicy sausages and mash the menu offers some interestingly different meals – the selection we were offered included ratatouille with goat's cheese or Stilton, rabbit and wild mushroom terrine and grilled duck breast with green peppercorn sauce.

Opening times during the week are from 12 noon to 3 pm and from 6 pm to 11 pm. Saturdays the inn is open from 12 noon to 4.30 pm and from 6 pm to 11 pm. Sundays the inn is open from 12 noon to 5 pm and from 7 pm to 10.30 pm. Meals are served from 12 noon to 2 pm and from 7 pm to 9.30 pm. Children are welcome until 8 pm and so are well-behaved dogs on leads. Telephone: 01730 827205.

The Walk

① With your back to the pub entrance turn right down the lane into the village.

Leave the green on your right and bear left at the junction, following the sign for Oakshott, Prior's Dean and Wheatham.

② After about 50 yards turn right along a concrete track, following the bridleway sign. This passes garages and becomes a narrow path with a field on the left and a hedge on the right. The path climbs gently up the field towards the wooded hanger and runs through a tunnel-like entrance into the trees to a signpost.

③ Turn right and follow the woodland path along the foot of the hanger. Tangled woods of beech and yew wreathed in wild clematis clothe the steep slope on your left. Follow the path, keeping mainly to the edge of the wood, for about 3/4 mile until just after a right-hand bend the path divides.

④ Keep straight ahead (left-hand path) to climb the side of the hanger. This wild country is popular with badgers as they can tunnel under the soft earth around the yew tree roots. At the top, the path curves left to emerge from the trees into an open field.

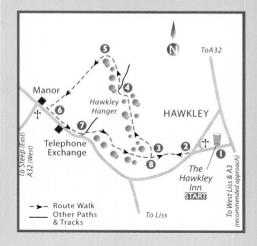

Hawkley village.

⑤ Follow the side of the field with woods, then a hedge, on your right. At the end of the field keep straight on down a narrow path (possibly a little overgrown) between hedges for just a few yards, then follow the side of a field, hedge on the right, down a wide grassy path into the valley. A church and manor house are on your right.

⑥ When you come to the lane turn left for about ¼ mile past a telephone exchange to a bridleway sign on the left just before the lane drops downhill.

⑦ Take this path to walk through the trees along the top of the hanger. The path curves right then left a little uphill to leave the trees. Continue across a small field to

PLACES OF INTEREST NEARBY
The Wakes, Selborne, to the north of Hawkley. This was the home of Gilbert White, author of the delightful The Natural History and Antiquities of Selborne. Opening times vary. Telephone: 01420 511275.

walk downhill through woods once more. On your right the trees part to give wonderful valley views. Pass a path on the right to meet our earlier path at the entrance to the woods.

⑧ Retrace your steps beside the field with the hedge on your left, turning left along the lane into the village and right to return to the pub and your car.

East Meon
Ye Olde George Inn

MAP: OS PATHFINDER 1265 (GR 680222) ⬩ **WALK 28** ⬩ **DISTANCE:** 1¼ OR 2¼ MILES

DIRECTIONS TO START: EAST MEON IS ABOUT 6 MILES WEST OF PETERSFIELD. APPROACH VIA THE A272 FROM PETERSFIELD OR WINCHESTER. YE OLDE GEORGE INN IS AT THE FOOT OF CHURCH STREET ADJACENT TO THE HIGH STREET. **PARKING:** PATRONS MAY LEAVE CARS IN THE PUB CAR PARK WHILE THEY WALK (ASK PERMISSION FIRST). ALTERNATIVELY, USE THE PUBLIC CAR PARK NEARBY.

A beautiful old-world village, a 15th century inn and a magnificent downland walk combine to make this a really memorable outing. The village of East Meon, with its splendid Norman church, medieval Court House, and rows of colourwashed houses and cottages, some thatched and timber-framed, others elegantly Georgian, is one of Hampshire's treasures. Its setting is equally lovely among softly curving hills. Our route crosses undulating farmland before climbing to the top of a ridge with breathtaking views over the Meon valley. We return to the village along a terraced woodland path. The climb to the top of the ridge is short but steep and you may prefer the shorter walk which avoids the climb.

Ye Olde George Inn

Whichever walk you choose you must not miss a visit to Ye Old George Inn. Huge open fires, old pine tables and benches, and walls adorned with pictures and mementos of times past contribute to the warm welcome awaiting you. A pair of 15th century cottages have been converted into the restaurant area which retains the original inglenook fireplaces, exposed brickwork and massive beams. There is a separate non-smoking area. Walkers are specially welcome and the inn is dogs and children friendly. The range of traditional ales includes Badger Gold, Tanglefoot and Sussex. Cider is Blackthorn and there is a wide range of wines. When we called an interesting menu included chicken and walnut timbale, Barbary duck breast served with a wine and summerfruit dressing and scallop and prawn mornay.

Opening times Monday to Friday are from 12 noon to 3 pm and from 6 pm to 11 pm (Sundays 7 pm to 10.30 pm). On Saturdays the pub opens at 11 am. Food is served from 12 noon to 2.30 pm and from 7 pm to 9.30 pm.

There is an attractive patio and garden and a safe play area for children. The inn offers also accommodation. Telephone: 01730 823481.

The Walk

① Turn right from the main entrance to the pub, and turn right again at Barnards Corner.

② As the lane swings left, you pass Workhouse Lane leading to the public car park on the right. Continue up the lane

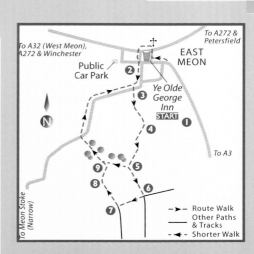

(Chapel Street) past the school and round a right-hand bend.

③ About 50 yards further, opposite Princes Cottages, turn left up the asphalted entrance to cross a parking area. Go through a gate and follow the path up the field ahead. Over on your right is a farmhouse and buildings. Cross a path to the farm and keep on with a hedge on your left.

④ When the hedge curves left, bear half-right as the sign directs to walk up an open field. The path may be indistinct but from the brow of the rise you will see our path descending to run just to the right of a tall hedge. Follow the path as it curves left then right uphill with the hedge on your left towards a belt of woodland. Cross the stile and bear right following the woodland path uphill to go through a gate.

For the shorter walk turn right with the trees on your right and keep ahead to go through the gate at point 9 and rejoin the longer walk.

The Cross, East Meon.

⑤ Turn left along the foot of the hillside with the trees on your left to a gate.

⑥ Do not go through the gate but turn right and climb the steep hillside with a fence on your left. As you climb a wonderful view unfolds to the east. Cross a stile and continue climbing to the top of the ridge.

⑦ At the gate, turn right along the ridge. The path descends slightly to a fence.

⑧ Bear right, with the fence on your left,

downhill to go through a gate. Keep on downhill to a gate leading into woodland on your left.

⑨ Turn left through the gate and follow a good path downhill through the woods to a lane. Turn right along the lane, rejoining our earlier route at the entrance to the parking area. Turn left down Workhouse Lane for the public car park. To see a pretty part of East Meon, leave the earlier route at Workhouse Lane and keep straight ahead along The Cross. Turn right across the stream in front of the cottages past the Izaak Walton pub then turn left up an alley to go through a gate. Cross a lane and follow the path with a wall on your left up a grassy track to the road. Turn left past the church, then turn left again to return to Ye Olde George Inn.

PLACES OF INTEREST NEARBY
East Meon village, particularly the church which has a magnificent 12th century black marble font from Tournai.

Buriton
The Five Bells

<table>
<tr><td>**MAP:** OS PATHFINDERS 1265, 1285
(GR 738202)</td><td>**WALK 29**</td><td>**DISTANCE:** 2 MILES</td></tr>
</table>

DIRECTIONS TO START: BURITON IS A MILE EAST OF THE A3, ABOUT 3 MILES SOUTH OF PETERSFIELD. THE VILLAGE IS SIGNED OFF THE A3. **PARKING:** DRIVE DOWN THE HIGH STREET AND PARK ON THE FAR SIDE OF THE POND IN FRONT OF THE CHURCHYARD WALL.

Some gentle climbing is involved in this walk but you will be rewarded by magnificent views over the South Downs and enjoy unspoilt countryside rich in rare trees, shrubs and flowers. South of Petersfield the chalk downland descends abruptly to greensand rocks, forming steep tree-covered hillsides known as 'hangers'. Nestling in their shadow you will find Buriton, an enchanting village built of the local cream-coloured malmstone. At the foot of the High Street streams rising in the chalk feed a large pond. It is now a happy playground for ducks but once it played an important part in village life, providing drink for the animals and a sheep-wash. Our walk starts from the pond, then takes an ancient track to the top of Buriton Hanger. An undulating route leads over the downs with a short detour to see a nature reserve before a quick descent brings us back to the village – the 2-mile distance for this walk allows for a stroll around this delightful place.

The Five Bells

A short distance up the High Street you will find this attractive 17th century inn, built of the local stone around a sunny courtyard. The cosy, cottage-style interior is full of character with comfortable padded window seats and homely wooden tables and chairs. At quiet times you may glimpse the Grey Lady. I was told she is a kindly ghost in peasant dress. From the extensive menu home-made pies are always popular and other favourite dishes include pan fried duck breast, Scottish sirloin steak and Cornish roasted sea bass. Real ales are Badger First Gold, Tanglefoot and Fursty Ferret. Opening times are from 11.30 am (Sundays from 12 noon) to 3 pm and from 5.30 pm to 11 pm. Meals are served from 12 noon to 2 pm (Sundays 2.30 pm) and from 6 pm to 9 pm.

Dogs are welcome and there is a pleasant garden. Accommodation is available in the Five Bells 'Cotts'. These are converted barns and stables, originally used to stable the horses and rest the cattlemen before making the last 3 mile drive to Petersfield market. Telephone: 01730 263584.

The Walk

① With the pond on your right and the church and churchyard wall on your left follow the gravel track beside the wall to the point where it curves left. Leave the track here and turn right to cross a stile into the meadows. Turn left along the foot of the meadows with a fence on your left. (This official diversion differs slightly from the OS map.) On your right the meadows slope up to the trees of Buriton

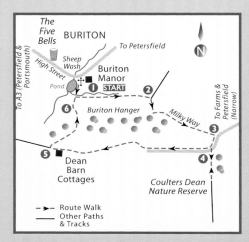

Hanger. Continue over stiles to a crossing track.

② Turn right to follow this ancient trackway, the Milky Way, as it winds upwards, through the tangled woods of the hanger. As the track levels near the top the trees part to give wonderful views. Continue past a track on the left to a tarmac lane.

③ Bear right along the lane to a sharp right-hand bend.

④ Make a short detour here along the footpath straight ahead to see Coulters Dean Nature Reserve. There is a splendid view of the reserve from a grassy area a short distance along the path. In summer the carpet of wildflowers includes eleven varieties of orchid. Among the butterflies they attract are the Brown Argus and the rare Duke of Burgundy. Retrace your steps to the lane and bear left downhill. The track becomes gravelled as it climbs the other side of the valley. Keep to the track as it winds over shallow downland valleys for almost a mile to meet a tarmac lane. Follow

Buriton from the path to the Hanger.

the lane to pass some cottages at Dean Barn and enter woodland.

⑤ About 100 yards after the cottages, you will see a footpath sign on the right, pointing down the side of the hanger. Turn

PLACES OF INTEREST NEARBY

The Queen Elizabeth Country Park offers over 1,000 acres of dramatic forest and downland with many trails for walkers, horse riders and cyclists and a wide range of other activities, as well as a visitor centre and the Coach House Café. Also Butser Ancient Farm. Telephone: 023 9259 5040.

right to follow the zig-zag path descending the hanger to a stile leading to the meadow we crossed at the beginning of the walk.

⑥ Climb the stile and bear half-right down the meadow to cross the stile in front of the churchyard wall. Retrace your steps, bearing left then right with the pond on your left to return to your car. If you have time, visit the beautiful 12th century church which is full of interest. In the Manor beside the church Edward Gibbon wrote part of his classic work *The Decline and Fall of the Roman Empire*.

Finchdean
The George

MAP: OS PATHFINDER 1285 (GR 739127)   WALK 30   DISTANCE: 3 MILES

DIRECTIONS TO START: FINCHDEAN IS 2 MILES NORTH OF ROWLANDS CASTLE. THE BEST APPROACH IS VIA THE A3. HEADING NORTH, TURN FOR HORNDEAN AND AFTER ABOUT A MILE TURN RIGHT FOR FINCHDEAN. HEADING SOUTH, TURN FOR CHALTON, DRIVE THROUGH THE VILLAGE, THEN FOLLOW THE SIGNS FOR FINCHDEAN. THE GEORGE OVERLOOKS THE GREEN. **PARKING:** PATRONS MAY LEAVE THEIR CARS IN THE PUB CAR PARK WHILE THEY WALK – PLEASE ASK FIRST. ALTERNATIVELY, THERE ARE SPACES BY THE GREEN.

This is a walk with everything: fine views, beautiful downland and woods, and a splendid pub. And tiny Finchdean is a delight. Hidden away in a tranquil valley, a cluster of homely houses and cottages surround a small green shaded by trees and bright with flowers. In spite of the railway close by, nowhere could be more peaceful! But in the 19th century the scene must have been very different. The attractive houses on the green were part of a brass and iron foundry producing agricultural machinery and the lane that winds dreamily past them was once a main coaching route from Portsmouth to London. Travellers alighted from the coaches to find rest and refreshment at the George and the same warm welcome awaits us today.

The George

Describing itself as an 18th century ale house, this is a small, friendly, traditional village pub, well-maintained and comfortable with a happy, relaxed atmosphere. Opening times on Monday to Saturday are 11 am to 3 pm and 6 pm to 11 pm; on Sundays 12 noon to 10.30 pm. Excellent home-cooked food is served at lunchtimes from 12 noon to 2 pm and evenings from 7 pm to 10 pm. When we called the menu included a delicious steak and kidney pudding, breast of chicken in tarragon and cream and duck in fruits of the forest sauce. Real ales are Bass and Youngs and there is always a guest ale. Cider and a range of wines are also on offer.

Dogs are welcome and there is a covered patio and pretty garden with a safe play area for children. The George is very popular with walkers so it is a good plan to ring beforehand to book your meal. Telephone: 023 9241 2257.

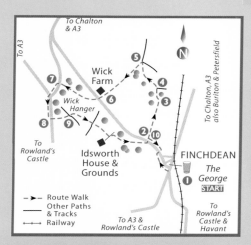

The Walk

① With your back to the pub entrance follow the lane ahead, signed 'Staunton Way, Queen Elizabeth Country Park'. Just past Ashcroft Lane turn right by the footpath sign, then turn left to resume your original heading along the foot of a field with a hedge on your left.

② At the end of the field turn right to walk uphill with a hedge still on your left. As you climb look back for a charming view of Finchdean nestling among the trees. When the hedge ceases keep straight on across an open field towards a wood. In the valley on the right you will see the

walled garden which once surrounded Old Idsworth House. In the 19th century it was the home of the local landowners, the Clark Jarvis family. They agreed to sell land in the valley to the railway company on condition a new house was built for them on top of Wick Hanger, over a mile away. We shall glimpse the new house later in our walk. All that remains of Idsworth is the church which you will see all by itself in a field.

③ Keep ahead with trees on your left, then through a more wooded area to a crossing track in front of an open field.

④ Turn left with the field on your right and trees on your left, still walking uphill. After about 200 yards bear right across the open field. On your left there is a glorious view over Langstone Harbour. Continue with a wood now on your left to a crossing track.

⑤ Turn left to keep the wood at first on your left and follow the grassy path downhill which finally tunnels between hedges to pass Wick Farm and bring you to a lane.

Finchdean.

⑥ Cross the road and take the track ahead which curves right to climb through the trees of Wick Hanger to a lane.

⑦ Turn left along the lane to a T-junction. Turn left again and follow the lane for about ¼ mile to a footpath sign on your left.

PLACES OF INTEREST NEARBY
Sir George Staunton Country Park, south of Rowland's Castle. Beautiful landscaped grounds, woodland walks and farm with rare breeds. Open every day, from 10 am to 5 pm between Good Friday and the end of September, rest of year 10 am to 4 pm. Telephone: 023 9245 3405.

⑧ Bear left as the sign directs and continue with woods on your left. At the corner of the wood follow the path straight ahead over a field to cross a stile leading into woods.

⑨ Follow the path over a crossing track to walk downhill, bearing right through the trees past the grounds of Idsworth House. Continue over a crossing track to a T-junction. Turn left. The track curves right and continues downhill. On the right across a clearing you can glimpse the ornate rooftop of Idsworth House.

⑩ When you reach the lane, turn right to retrace your steps to Finchdean.